THE ZWEMER DIARIES

THE ZWEMER DIARIES

1888

The New Brunswick Years

Edited and transcribed by

Matthew Gasero

THE BEARDSLEE PRESS
New Brunswick, New Jersey

New Brunswick Theological Seminary
35 Seminary Place, New Brunswick, NJ 08901

Printed in the United States of America

ISBN 13: 978-1-7327952-0-4
ISBN 10: 1-7327952-0-7

Library of Congress Control Number: 2018911027

"*The printed page is a missionary that can go anywhere and do so at minimum cost. It enters closed lands and reaches all strata of society. It does not grow weary. It needs no furlough. It lives longer than any missionary. It never gets ill. It penetrates through the mind to the heart and conscience. It has and is producing results everywhere. It has often lain dormant yet retained its life and bloomed years later.*"

Samuel Marinus Zwemer

Samuel Marinus Zwemer's signature
at the end of his diary.

Contents

Illustrations

Abbreviations Used

AMF   Mrs. T.C. Rounds, Editor, *American Messianic Fellowship Monthly*, The Jewish Era Vol 7 No 2, Chicago, IL, 1898.

Corwin   Edward Tanjore Corwin. *A Manual of the Reformed Church in America, 1628–1902*. Board of Publication of the Reformed Church in America, New York, NY. 1902.

HD   Russell L. Gasero, *Historical Directory of the Reformed Church in America, 1628–2000*. Wm. B. Eerdmans Publishing Co. Grand Rapids, MI. 2000.

MH   www.myheritage.org

PTS   Joseph H. Dulles, *Princeton Theological Seminary Biographical Catalogue*, Trenton, NJ, 1909.

Raven   John Howard Raven. *Biographical Record: Theological Seminary, New Brunswick, 1784-1934*. New Brunswick Theological Seminary, New Brunswick, NJ. 1934.

Rutgers John Howard Raven. *Catalogue of the Officers and Alumni of Rutgers College in New Brunswick, New Jersey, 1766–1916*. State Gazette Publishing Co., Printers, Trenton, NJ, 1916.

UTS   Union Theological Seminary Alumni Catalogue, 1836–1936, New York, NY, 1937.

WC   Twenty-Eighth Annual Register of Wheaton College, Cincinnati, OH, 1888.

WTS   Western Theological Seminary "1899–1900 Catalog"

Launch of Beardslee Press

Rev. Dr. Micah McCreary

Welcome to Beardslee Press, a newly-established resource of New Brunswick Theological Semnary (NBTS). NBTS is a seminary grounded in Jesus Christ and empowered by the Holy Spirit to participate in God's reign on earth. We are proudly rooted in the Reformed tradition and centered in its trust of God's sovereignty and grace. We are an intercultural, ecumenical school of Christian faith and scholarship, committed to metro-urban and global contexts.

Our mission is to educate individuals and strengthen communities for life-changing public ministries in church and society. We fulfill this mission through creative, contextual, and critical engagement with texts, traditions, and practices. Our vision is to shape seminarians with a calling to God's cities, spiritual vitality, and community transformation!

Beardslee Press is an entity of the Reformed Church Center at New Brunswick Theological Seminary - a place where:

- future Reformed Church in America (RCA) ministers are educated and developed. RCA students are encouraged to have a strong sense of belonging in the RCA. They are taught how to connect with others, to understand the foundation of the denomination, and to execute their ministries through workshops and events within the seminary community that help them connect with the life of the denomination.

· the Reformed Church is able to speak to the Seminary. This oldest seminary in North America is a rich and diverse learning community, with roots in the RCA. The Center is at the intersection of that past and its present, and provides opportunities for the Seminary community to learn ways in which the best of the RCA speaks to the whole Church.

· there is space to think about what it means to be Reformed. The voice of the RCA is most vital when it is continually being renewed. That requires reflection and discussion and a space to share ideas freely, while informed by a variety of backgrounds, cultures, and worldviews. The richness of faith and culture in the modern NBTS helps the Center encourage and sponsor reflection on the living traditions of the RCA, as well as on the issues that now face the RCA, drawing on the resources of this community, in which both free inquiry and disciplined analysis are deeply valued.

The Reformed Church Center offers a broad range of programs for a wide audience, including scholars, RCA members, and everyone concerned about the Reformed tradition and its continued renewal. Beardslee Press will become a resource for and instrument of the Seminary. There has been a deep desire by the Office of the President at NBTS to start a press through the Reformed Church Center. The 2018 NBTS Founders Day provides a meaningful opportunity to launch this valuable entity as NBTS celebrates its founding and its close relationship with the Reformed Church in America.

We have strategically chosen to name our publishing resource in honor of the Beardslee family, four generations of whom served the RCA in ministry, while three generations taught at this Seminary.

· John Walter Beardslee (1837-1921) was born in Sandusky, Ohio, and baptized in New Fairfield, Connecticut. Je graduated from Rutgers College in 1860 and NBTS in 1863—he went on to receive both a D.D. (1884) and an L.L.D. (1907) from Rutgers. He served as a pastor in Constantine, Michigan, 1864-1884, and West Troy, New York, 1884-1888. He became a professor at Western Theological Seminary in Holland, Michigan, in

1888, and remained there until 1917. In 1913 the library at Western Seminary was named Beardslee Memorial Library on the occasion of his twenty-fifth year as a professor there. He was on the faculty at NBTS from 1917 until his death at the age of eighty-four.

- John Walter Beardslee, Jr., (1879-1962) was born in Constantine, Michigan. at NBTS 1917-49; He was educated at Hope College, Western Seminary, and at the University of Chicago (M.A. and Ph.D). His teaching career of forty-four years included Hope College (1905-13), Western Seminary (1913-1917), and New Brunswick Theological Seminary (1917-49), where he also served as president (1935-1947). Upon his retirement at age seventy, he continued as a part-time teacher and acting dean until 1955, rendering fifty years of service. His wife, Frances, was also an accomplished Greek scholar who tutored generations of students at both Western and New Brunswick and was one of the leaders in the fight for women's ordination to all offices of the RCA.

- John Walter Beardslee, III, (1914-2001) was born in Holland, Michigan, and educated at Yale University (A.B. 1935 and Ph.D. 1957), and Princeton Theological Seminary (1941). His teaching tenure included positions in Basrah, Iraq (1935-38), Annville Institute in Kentucky (1943-44), George Washington University (1948-51), Central College (1951-64), and New Brunswick Theological Seminary (1964-84). A pastor for two years (First Reformed Church, Tarrytown, New York), his teaching tenure extended into his retirement, as interim director of Gardner Sage Library and advisor to students until near the time of his death, a total os sixty-five years. He was volunteer Archivist for the Reformed Church in America, one of the first members of the Commission on History of the RCA, and, as part of that Commission, responsible for the hiring of a professional Archivist and the creation of *The Historical Series of the Reformed Church in America*. He was also known as a passionate voice for social justice.

In addition to these three members of our faculty, William Armitage Beardslee (1867-1897), a second William Armitage Beardslee (1916-2001), Frank Palmer Beardslee (1918-1975) and Nancy Eunice Beardslee (who still lives in New Brunswick) have all served as RCA ministers. The second William Beardslee was also a New Testament scholar, teaching at Emory University and Columbia Theological Seminary.

Our first publication from Beardslee Press focuses on the the seminary career of Samuel Marinus Zwemer (April 12, 1867 – April 2, 1952), American missionary, traveler, and scholar who was often called The Apostle to Islam. A native of Vriesland, Michigan, he received an A.B. from Hope College in Holland, Michigan, in 1887 , and an M.A. from New Brunswick Theological Seminary in 1890.

After being ordained to the Reformed Church ministry by the Classis of Pella, Iowa, in 1890, he became one of the founding members of the Arabian Mission and served as a missionary in Busrah, Bahrein, and other locations in Arabia from 1891 to 1905. Zwemer served in Egypt from 1913 to 1929, and also traveled widely in Asia Minor, where he was elected a fellow of the Royal Geographical Society of London.

In 1929 he was appointed Professor of Missions and professor of the History of Religion at the Princeton Theological Seminary, where he taught until 1937. He founded and edited the publication *The Moslem World* for 35 years and was influential in mobilizing many Christians to serve as missionaries in Islamic countries. Zwemer retired from the faculty of Princeton Theological Seminary at the age of seventy, but continued to write and publish books and articles as well as doing a great deal of public speaking. Zwemer died in New York City at the age of eighty-four.

This Beardslee Press book is a historical reprint of Zwemer's diary from 1888. This and subsequent volumes provide insight into how he and a fellow missionary student, James Cantine, jointly established the Arabian Mission—an endeavor they solely implanted and led for a decade before releasing its administration to the RCA . Zwemer's diary reveals the mindset, motivation, and actions of an indefatigable fundraiser, a visionary in mission theory and practice, even as a first-year student at NBTS. It is fitting to launch Beardslee Press with the story of such a person as Zwemer, who was known personally by John W. Beardslee, III.

Zwemer Diaries Project

Adam Simnowitz

I am thrilled to announce the start of the digitization of the Zwemer diaries[1] that were donated by his family. This valuable collection of the RCA Archives consists of 22 volumes spanning the years 1888-1925.[2] The diaries begin three and a half months after he entered New Brunswick Theological Seminary where the vision for the Arabian Mission was conceived and birthed,[3] until the time he had been well established as "one of the leading authorities on everything pertaining to Islam."[4]

Samuel Marinus Zwemer, arguably the RCA's most prominent son and America's greatest missionary to Muslims, has almost been

---

[1] Zwemer and his family referred to these books as his diaries. They are actually date books that contain a combination of personal reflections, appointments, and accomplishments for a given day.

[2] This collection lacks the following: Aug. 12, 1892 - July 9, 1893; Nov. 25, 1894 -1899; 1901-1905; 1911-12; 1915-1916.

[3] See entry for November 23, 1888.

[4] Anonymous, *Methodist Review*, vol. 98, September 1916, 828.

[5] John R. Mott, Addresses and Papers of John R. Mott, volume one: The Student Volunteer Movement for Foreign Missions, (New York: Association Press, 1946), 123, 144.

completely forgotten by evangelicals since his passing in 1952. Among those who do remember him, Zwemer is a shining example of missions to Muslims. In addition to helping start the Arabian Mission, with all of its ministry in evangelistic, medical, and educational work, Zwemer, through his life, lectures, and literature, was responsible for instilling missions to Muslims into the consciousness of thousands of Christians around the world.

This rich legacy is perhaps best exemplified by his participation in the Student Volunteer Movement for Foreign Missions (SVMFM) initially as one of the first thousand volunteers and then as one of its leaders. John R. Mott, a founder of SVMFM and its long-time leader, wrote that the primary reason for the great increase in missionaries (eventually over 20,000) sailing from North America to serve overseas coincided with the establishment of the Candidates Department and Zwemer's role in it.[5] He also served as one of the primary key-note speakers at their quadrennial conventions and wrote several books as part of their curriculum to educate these prospective missionaries.[6]

Ironically, these and other such accomplishments have also earned for Zwemer a number of detractors. For instance, he is *still* vilified by a number of Muslims as their ultimate Christian nemesis.[7] Such a response is understandable towards him who during his lifetime was alternately referred to as "the Apostle to Islam" and "the Apostle to Muslims," considering that few things arouse Muslims' anger more than those who seek their conversion to Christianity. A less understandable faction are those professing evangelicals who disparage Zwemer as being a "product of his times" and a failure.[8] With the current growth of Islam and Muslims in non-Muslim nations, one would expect evangelicals to at least consider, if not be humble enough to learn from, one of their own who was once described by a leading German academic as "the world's leading authority on popular Islam from the standpoint of personal observation."[9]

[6] E.g. *Islam: a Challenge to Faith* (1907); *The Unoccupied Mission Fields of Africa and Asia* (1911).

[7] Heather J. Sharkey, *American Evangelicals in Egypt: Missionary Encounters in an Age of Empire* (Princeton: Princeton University Press, 2008), 94.

[8] Keith E. Swartley, *Encountering the World of Islam*, second ed. (Littleton, CO: Authentic, 2014) 332-334. The author misrepresents Zwemer as one who "verbally attacked Islam early in [his] career" who "later became [an] advocate of Christian witness" as well as implying from the context that he did not actually live among Muslims (332). He concludes that Zwemer and other early Christian missionaries to Muslims are people to be studied so as to "avoid their pitfalls" (334).

[9] J. Christy Wilson, *Apostle to Islam: a Biography of Samuel M. Zwemer*, 1952, 242.

Whether praised or despised, those who write about Zwemer often have one thing in common—*almost exclusive reliance on his published books about Islam and Muslims.* Occasionally, a few hardier researchers have referenced some of his articles from *The Moslem World* journal that he started and edited from 1911-1947. While these two sources are natural and convenient starting points, it only gives one aspect of Zwemer, namely his communication to fellow believers and missions colleagues about how to think about Islam and evangelize Muslims. As important as are published writings, it is usually in the personal papers and correspondence where we gain valuable insights into the thinking behind them.

With the anticipated completion of the Zwemer diaries project we will now have convenient access to materials that will help provide us with a fuller picture of the man, his work, and his legacy. It is also hoped that this project will spur a desire for a systematic digitization of other Zwemer materials, Arabian Mission materials, and other RCA historical records. The goal is to enable and spur serious research that will help us fairly view the past, to inspire us to obey the Two Greatest Commandments to love God and neighbor (Matt 22:34-40).

The following is a selected list of published and unpublished RCA materials relating to Zwemer, the Arabian Mission, and the Foreign Missions department, that I hope to see made available to researchers through their digitization:

Zwemer diaries (the final 21 volumes)
Zwemer papers
Arabian Mission records
Christian Intelligencer
Day Star
De Hope (Dutch)
De Heidenwereld (Dutch)
The Mission Field

The RCA Archives has been entrusted with many invaluable materials for all researchers. Along with this rich heritage comes an obligation to both God and the visible Church to provide us with access to His past faithfulness as we carry on in the present and look forward to the future.

Will you be the one to help underwrite the Zwemer diaries project and other related materials?

Foreword

Matthew Gasero

Samuel Zwemer, an important part of the missionary world in the late 1800's into the 1900's, who along with James Cantine and John Lansing, established the American Arabian Mission. In his journals one will get an intimate look into his life. His thoughts on missions, churches, their ministers, and colleagues are laid bare for the first time. In 1888, Samuel encounters a wide assortment of individuals—seminary students to world renowned ministers. He often writes his thoughts about an encounter or an individual. The best approach to this volume is to read it more than once. Samuel, on some occasions, appears as rather arrogant, and even a little pompous. Reading his diary a second time, may help you have a better understanding of his thought process, and some insight into his thinking.

This is the only publicly available copy of one of Samuel's diaries to date. The original journals of Samuel Zwemer are a closed collection located in the Reformed Church Archives. They are in a damaged but stable condition and as such are often difficult to read. A long-term project for the digitization and publication of his diaries is underway. Anyone may help fund this endeavor by donating to the Reformed Church Archives at: www.rca.org/give/archives-special-project

Every effort has been made to keep the transcription as close to the original wording and markings as possible. You will encounter the occasional misspelling and his tendency to underline only parts of words. This was transcribed to retain the original tone and emphasis Samuel may have intended. Samuel also often used his own form of short hand and abbreviations and rarely used first names when identifying people. Despite my best efforts to interpret Samuel's handwriting, there are instances where words and names are incomprehensible. In such cases they are left as close to how they appear and are marked with a note in brackets. It should be noted that on several pages vertical lines would be drawn down the margin, and some days will have an X next to the date—these have been removed for this transcription.

There are a few special people that made this task lighter and kept me focused on this result. I would like to thank my father, Russell Gasero, for the knowledge and fierce protection of the Reformed Church in America's heritage that has been an inspiration my entire life. Without him, this would not be possible. James Brumm a teacher turned colleague and I remember our trips to Dailey's Pond when I was a child with fondness. Dennis Bruno, a friend, a confidant, my brother and Brittany Zukow, my friend, and voice of reason. There are no words with which to thank you both. And finally, to Lindsey Stirling, your music was the fuel that kept this project moving forward.

And now, I present to you Samuel Marinus Zwemer's thoughts and feelings of 1888.

January 1888

January, Sunday 1. 1888.

Arose at 8.30. Attended Prayer Meeting at Med. Miss Training Institute. 118 E 45th St. New York. Breakfast with the boys & ladies. Went to Dr. J. Hall's[1] church & heard a fine sermon on missions text. Ps. 96:10 Congregational Singing. Took dinner. Went to Mission for Xtian Jews conducted by Rev. Freshman.[2] Had an interesting class of Jewish boys — regular heathen! Went from there to the Roosevelt St. Mission. One of the worst places in N.Y. Was insulted & thrown with dirt by one of the boys in my class. Took lunch at the Dispensary. Went to Bleecker St. Mission. Very pleasant meeting about 12 inquirers. Many promised to Reform. A Happy New Year's day!

♒

January, Monday 2. 1888.

Left Dr. Doucomt [sp?] at 9.30 Took 3rd Ave elevated car for Bowery. Walked to Ferry Took train for New Brunswick Spent P.M. in reading & writing.

Was invited to take supper at Dr. Lansing[3].

Spent a very pleasant evening seeing Egyptian curiosities etc.

Saw Photographs (taken from mummy) of Rameses I & II & of Seti I. Also coins & other things.

Went home at 10. & Retired at eleven.

My vacation days have been very pleasant.

Recd. A fine New Years Card from A. B. Reed & also from my sisters.

♒

January, Tuesday 3. 1888.

Spent A.M. In reading & writing letters to Father[4] & Sisters & Brother F.J.Z[5].

---

[1]   John Hall (1829-1898), Pastor, Fifth Avenue Presbyterian Church, 1867-1898.
[2]   Jacob Freshman (1842-1898), Missionary, New York City, NY. AMF, 47
[3]   John Gulian Lansing (1851-1906), Professor, New Brunswick Theological Seminary 1884-1898. Raven, 139
[4]   Adrian Zwemer (1823-1910), father of Samuel Zwemer, Pastor, Free Grace, Orange City, IA 1886-1891. HD, 481
[5]   Frederick James Zwemer (1858-1903), brother of Samuel Zwemer, Missionary, Classis of the Dakotas, 1887-92. HD, 481

Adrian Zwemer

Went up town & purchased a book-case & some other things for my room.

Spent P.M. In reading & studying.

Read Part of Revelation. What a glorious book full of promises.

Wrote to Miss A.B. Reed in Evening. Told her of the New York Mission'y society.

Read the Harpers for January. "Virginia of Virginia" is a fine story.

Retired at 12 M.

Enjoyed a season of prayer to-day. "Ah for a closer walk with God." It is only near Him that one is safe.

January, Wednesday 4. 1888.

Arose at 7.30 Attended all Recitations. Dr Woodbridge[6] spoke on the benefit of Symbols in preaching. Went up town & received a Registered package — a New Years present from home. A penwiper $2. & a long letter from Sister Rika.

---

[6]   Samuel Merrill Woodbridge (1819-1905), Professor, 1865-1901. Dean of Seminary, 1883-1888. President of Faculty, 1888-1901. New Brunswick Theological Seminary. Raven, 21

Spent afternoon in study. Recd. money in full from Rev. Nies[7] & sent same to J.F.Z[8].

Attended Prayer Meeting — Week of prayer — in 3ʳᵈ Ref. Church. Subject, Personal Work. A very good meeting. Spent a pleasant season of prayer in Mr. Andrew's[9] Room. Read Bible & Retired.

Weather to-day warm for January. No snow as yet.

ℨ

January, Thursday 5. 1888.

Arose at 7. Attended Recitations. Dr. De Witt[10] discussed John's Λογοσ[11] vs. Philo's. We came to the conclusion that John may have borrowed the word from Philo — the idea was new & transcendent. Received a letter from Brother P.J.Z.[12] Wrote to Passaic to get an agent for Father's book of poems.

Studied lessons. Read Greek according to custom with Rev. Willis[13] from 5:30-6. Exercised in Gymnasium Attended Evening Prayers. "[ditto — Attended] New Brunswick Choral Society. Read Bible & Retired.

Very pleasant day. Sorry I could not attend Prayer Meeting this evening.

ℨ

January, Friday 6. 1888.

Arose at 7.00 Read Bible Attended Recitations. Handed Essay on Apostles Creed to Dr. Mabon[14].

---

[7] Helenus Elizaus Nies (1844-1923), Pastor, Union, Paterson, NJ, 1880-1910. HD, 287
[8] James Frederick Zwemer (1850-1921) brother of Samuel Zwemer, Agent, Western Institutions, 1888-90. HD, 481
[9] Lewis Curry Andrew (1852-1938), New Brunswick Theological Seminary, 1890. HD, 8
[10] John De Witt (1821-1906), Professor, New Brunswick Theological Seminary, 1863-1892. HD, 103
[11] Λογοσ [logos]: Word, Discourse, or Reason. Meant as the word of God.
[12] Peter John Zwemer (1869-1898), brother of Samuel Zwemer. AB, Hope, 1888. HD, 481
[13] Ralph Willis (1815-1895), Rector of Hertzog Hall, New Brunswick Theological Seminary, 1880-88. HD, 467
[14] William Augustus Van Vranken Mabon (1882-92), Professor, New Brunswick Theological Seminary, 1881-92. HD, 246

Studied lessons & wrote to Brother Peter. Wrote article for "De Hope" on Missions. Expect to write an article for above paper every week. Spent evening in study & conversation.

❧

January, Saturday 7. 1888.

Spent day in Study & writing. Read Book of Numbers.

Wrote essay on "The Connection of The Old & New Testaments" for Dr. Woodbridge.

Showed their connection by Design, Symbolism, Prophecy Quotations. Hist. Of Jews & the subject of both — Christ. Attended meeting of choir. Read & studied in evening. Enjoyed a season of prayer today.

God is always nearer than we think if we will only call upon Him.

❧

January, Sunday 8. 1888.

Arose at 7.00 attended service in 4th Ref. Church. Dr. Mabon on words "Ye are not your own." Consecration service. Good. Attended S.S. Meeting. Seven in my class. Lesson on Feeding The Multitude.

Went to Union Communion Service (after week of prayer) of all the denominations of the city — held in 2nd Ref. Church. Very impressive service "<u>One</u> Lord, <u>One</u> Faith One Baptism."

Went to Throop Ave. Mission after tea.

Led the Meeting. Subject: The Good Shepherd. About 60 were present. No Inquirers. Walked home with Hieber[15]. Had a talk with Andrew about Mission-work in the West. Retired.

A Very pleasant Sabbath.

❧

January, Monday 9. 1888.

Attended Recitations in A.M. & read commentaries for my sermon. Received a postal from Fred - J.Z. — very cold in Dakota 20 below zero. Here it is 30 above.

Exercised in the Gymnasium. Attended Preaching in Chapel. Mr. Tilton[16] text "Search the Scriptures" Very good delivery but

---

[15]   Louis Hieber, (1863-1908), Rutgers College, 1888-89. HD, 175
[16]   Edgar Tilton Jr. (1865-1954), New Brunswick Theological Seminary, 1889. HD, 397

commonplace sermon. Went to Rehearsal of musical association in
Y.M.C.A. Hall. Read Bible — Timothy until 12 M. Retired. Weather fine
& warm.

ჳ

January, Tuesday 10. 1888.

Arose at 8.00 & missed my breakfast. Attended Recitations
Hebrew Dr. Lansing
Methodology Dr. Mabon.
Preaching Dr. Demarest[17].
Mr. Andrews preached on "Resurrection" — a good argumentative
sermon but not practical enough. No thought for the sinner. Delivery
good.

Spent P.M. in study. Prepared essay for the Mission-Band on
Life of John Williams[18] — what a glorious life — a martyr death — a
golden crown. Read his book on Polynesia. Mr. Wijkhoff[19] was present.
Commenced to write sermon on John. 4:10 — My first effort. I hope it
may be a first-fruits acceptable to my Master.

Retired at 11.30 P.M. Weather fine & warm.

ჳ

January, Wednesday 11. 1888.

Attended Recitations.
Read & Studied.
Attended Preaching by Mr. Phelps[20] in the evening. Very good
sermon on Xtian Benevolence. Text: the history of the widow's mite.
Very earnest in language but not strong in delivery.

Attended meeting of Soc. of Inquiry. Heard papers on Church
Music & on the Episcopal Church. Acted as Sect'y.

Went to final rehearsal of Musical association. Very crowded
stage.

Retired at 11.30 after reading <u>Bible</u>.

---

[17]   David D. Demarest (1819-1898), trustee, Rutgers College, 1858-1898, Professor,
New Brunswick Theological Seminary, 1865-1898. HD, 96

[18]   John Williams (1796-1839), Missionary, London Missionary Society. *Britannica* 15th
Ed. v9, 944

[19]   Charles Sterling Wyckoff (1866-1945), Rutgers College, 1888. HD, 474

[20]   Philip Tertius Phelps (1862-1944), New Brunswick Theological Seminary, 1889.
HD, 306

Frank Seymour Scudder

♫

January, Thursday 12. 1888.

Arose at 7. Attended Recit. at 9 A. M. Studied. Attended Instruction in Elocution by Prof. Peabody[21] in P.M. Gave a Prayer Meety talk on John 10. Exercised in Gymnasium. Attended 1st Concert given by the "N.B. Musical Association.

Program very good. Sang 1st Bass in the Chorus. Received letter notifying me of my appointment as one of the visitors of the Alliance formed by the churches for a Christian canvass of all the families of the town. I hope this movement will do much good. But I fear it is too much machinery for such a work.

Retired at 12.00.

♫

January, Friday 13. 1888.

Attended Recitations.

Dr. Mabon spoke on the different lives of Christ & recommended Edersheims as one of the best.

---

[21] Stephen George Peabody (1830-1898), Instructor, New Brunswick Theological Seminary, 1865-67 Raven, 42

Spent P.M. in study. Attended a meeting of the New Brunswick Christian Alliance in the 4ᵗʰ Ref. Ch.

Dr. Mabon addressed us. Called on Miss. Willis & notified her of her appointment as one of the visitors. Went to Bethel Mission in evening with Frank Scudder[22]. Small audience but a pleasant time. Recd. letter from Sister Mary.

Studied & Read.

Retired at 12.30 A.M.

♃

January, Saturday 14. 1888.

Arose at 7.30. Breakfast. Oh how sin draws us away from His presence. Came back in prayer. Wrote at sermon. Finished it before dinner. Went to Library & got several books on Missions.

The Gardener A. Sage Library[23] has 49,500 volumes.

Exercised in Gymnasium. Read Greek with Rev. Willis Matthew's Gospel.

Attended Choir Meeting. Read Bible & Retired. Oh that our prayer might always be "Oh for a closer walk with God"

Discussed to-day at the dinner table whether the need for workers was greater in the home than in the foreign field.

When will the boys see that a soul in Afrika = one in America!

But they fail to see it.

♃

January, Sunday 15. 1888.

Rainy & Muddy. Attended church in A.M. Dr. Campbell[24] "Let Brotherly Love continue" Very eloquent. Home strikes. "Oh how these Xtians love one another". Would that we might have more Xtian unity. Took dinner at Dr. Mabons. Pleasant time. Mrs. Mabon is a fine motherly sort of woman. Dr. Campbell in P.M. "Be not slothful to follow.....who through faith have inherited the promises." Good sermon an "Example". He spoke of Jerry Mc Auley[25]. S.S. class 8. Pleasant time. Lesson on Peter's Faith.

[22] Frank Seymour Scudder (1862-1956), New Brunswick Theological Seminary, 1890. HD, 352
[23] Gardner A. Sage Library built in 1875 for New Brunswick Theological Seminary.
[24] William Henry Campbell (1808-1890), Pastor, Suydam St, New Brunswick, NJ, 1883-1890. HD, 63
[25] Jerry Mc Auley (1839-1884), Rescue Mission Founder.

Attended Prayer Meeting: "Trust" Remained at home in evening read Deuteronomy. & Mission Papers by Lowrie[26]. Very good. Retired at 10 P.M. Very tired. Spent a blessed Sabbath-day.

ॐ

January, Monday 16. 1888.

Attended Recitations as usual.
Wrote a letter to H.V.S Peeke[27].

ॐ

January, Tuesday 17. 1888.

Arose at 6.30 Studied. Attended Recitations.
Dr. Mabon commended my essay. Read & Studied in P.M. Wrote a letter to sister Mary. Exercised in the Gymnasium. Chest measure to-day 38 1/8 in. weight 154# & height 5:11 1/8 ft.
Attended Meeting of Mission Band. Very Interesting. Mr. Scudder led the meeting. Was appointed Secty. & Treasurer.
Spent evening in reading & writing.
Weather cold. 15°.
Rain & warmer towards evening.

ॐ

January, Wednesday 18. 1888.

Attended Recitations as usual.
Led Prayer Meeting. "Ye are my witnesses".
Studied. Gymnasium.
Recited Greek: Math 24. Commenced to study Hartshornes[28] Conspectus v [of] Med. Science.
Read Joshua & part of Judges to-day.
Wrote letter to Prof. Lorsett & to Mr. Wilder[29] of Princeton.
Spoke with Phelps on the practicability of holding a Miss'y

---

26 Likely Walter Macon Lowrie (1819-1847), Missionary to China.
27 Harmon Van Slyke Peeke (1866-1929), New Brunswick Theological Seminary, 1891. HD, 302
28 Henry Hartshorne (1823-1897), Doctor, Founder of American Public Health Association, 1872.
29 Robert Parmelee Wilder (1863-1938), Union Seminary, 1891. UTS, 146

Conference here of Union, Princeton & Lancaster Seminaries. Expect to carry it out if possible.

♩

January, Thursday 19. 1888.

Attended Recitations.

Attended Lectures on Elocution by Prof. Peabody of Princeton. Read Rom. 8.

Studied & wrote letters to the boys at Lancaster Seminary & Crozer Seminary to see about the practicability of holding a Missionary Alliance at N.B. Wrote to Philip Sarlen, about our College Paper.

Exercised in the Gymnasium. Recited Greek. Studied Sermon. Read Medicine & Read book of Judges & part of I Samuel. Did not study my Bible enough last year but hope to do better this year.

The book of Judges is full of illustrations & curious texts. Recd. Letter from M. Ossewaarde[30] in relation to the American Bible Society.

♩

January, Friday 20. 1888.

[No Entry]

♩

January, Saturday 21. 1888.

Called on Dr. Campbell to day. Had a pleasant talk with him on Missions. Recd. Postal from Jas F. telling of the terrible Blizzard in Dakota & Iowa[31] — hundreds of lives lost! by exposure to the cold.

Coal famine in Kansas.

9°+ in New Brunswick & very little snow.

♩

January, Sunday 22. 1888.

Arose at 7.00 Dressed. Breakfast. Read Bible until Church time. Heard good sermon by the Old Doctor. on Xtian Fellowship. Very cold day thermometer..-3°.

---

[30] Martin Ossewaarde (1865-1916), Hope College, 1888. Raven, 162
[31] The Schoolchildren's Blizzard of 1888. See Beccy Tanner, *The Wichita Eagle*, December 31, 2012. https://www.kansas.com/news/local/news-columns-blogs/the-story-of-kansas/article1105618.html

Attended S.S. in P.M. & church Heard Sermon by Campbell on Xtian Endeavor. Prayer Meeting led by Sharpley[32] Recd. Letter from F.J.Z. telling of his narrow escape from freezing to death on Jan 13th 88.

Read it to the boys.

Recd. several letters from R.P. Wilder on Missions. Attended Domestic Mission Meeting in 2nd Ref. Ch. & heard a ridiculous account of domestic missions in Iowa by Dr. Hutton[33]. How ignorant "The East" is of the <u>Western</u> Church.

$$\mathcal{Z}$$

January, Monday 23. 1888.

Read Bible. Wrote letters. studied sermon. Recd. letter from Nellie with $6 inclosed and also the first no. v [of] 1 [the] Missy. Review v [of] 1 [the] world. Attended Recitations. Read letter from F.J.Z. To Dr. Woodbridge & Dr. Mabon.

Studied in evening & wrote letters.

Read Bible I Samuel & II Samuel. Davids history is very instructive. Retired at 11.30 P.M.

$$\mathcal{Z}$$

January, Tuesday 24. 1888.

Arose at 7.00 A.M. Studied & Preached <u>my first</u> sermon. John 4:10 Was criticised on some grammatical faults & because I omitted one petition from the Lords Prayer.

For the rest I was happily calm in my delivery & Dr. Demarest said it was "a good first effort"!

I expect to change it as soon as I have time & opportunity.

Attended Meeting of the Mission Band. Acted as secty. Got an idea into my head that our Seminary ought to send its own Missy to the foreign field at 7.30 P.M. Spoke to Phelps. Raised 150$ before 11 P.M. Among 1 [the] faculty & boys v [of] 1 [the] Seminary. God has blessed also this effort of mine.

---

[32]   Giles Herbert Sharpley (1864-1952), New Brunswick Theological Seminary, 1889. Raven, 163

[33]   Mancius Holmes Hutton (1837-1909), Pastor, Second, New Brunswick, NJ, 1879-1907, President, General Synod, 1888. HD, 191

♀

January, Wednesday 25. 1888.

Attended Recitations.

Did some more collecting now nearly $200. I hope we can raise $1700 by Thursday evening & send out our man in May. Attended Prayer Meety.

Wrote letters to all the Seminaries in New York New Jersey & Penn. To invite them to a District Miss'y Alliance at New Brunswick on Feb 24ᵗʰ next.

Went out collecty money with Philip Phelps. Raised about $75 more.

Society of Inquiry in evening. Good Meeting. Read & Retired early.

♀

January, Thursday 26. 1888.

Day of Prayer for Colleges. Remained at home with F.S. Scudder who was sick. Attended Meeting in P.M. led by Jno. Allen[34] of the Senior class at the Seminary. Lively meeting.

At an after meeting the sum for our own Missionary was raised to $550. I subscribed $10 yearly. Studied & read in evening. Wrote to "De Hope" & to the boys at Holland

Very pleasant day. A little warmer outside & in my heart.

Oh that the boys at all the different Seminaries would awake & consecrate themselves unreservedly to God's Service.

Paul calls himself a "δουλοσ"[35] of Jesus Xt. & can we not be the same.

♀

January, Friday 27. 1888.

Attended Recitations.

Dr. Mabon spoke against form & endless liturgy in church service. A simple service attracts the sinner more than cloth & gilt. Whitfield said: "When I first came to America they had wooden churches & golden preachers but now they have golden churches & wooden preachers".

---

[34] John Mitchell Allen (1861-1892), New Brunswick Theological Seminary, 1888. HD, 5
[35] δουλοσ [duolos]: a slave or servant

Heard Rev. G. Taylor[36] in the P. M. a very earnest speaker & city Missionary, at work in Hartford Connecticut. He addressed the Sem. boys for an hour this P.M. He recommends active laymen organization & more earnestness to win souls & less desire for Denominational glory. Read. Wrote to Maud[37] & retired at 11.00 P.M.

$$\mathcal{Z}$$

January, Saturday 28. 1888.

Studied all A.M. Wrote for "De Hope" on Missions Read & Studied in P.M.

Had a call from Mr. Merril[38] of Union Seminary. Received a Mission Chart as a present from Mr. Wilder of Union.

Bought some ink & mucilage today. Sent catalogue of Seminary to Miss A.B.R.

Went to choir-meeting; Saw moon-eclipse — nearly total at 7:15 P.M. Had a pleasant time at Dr. Mabon's.

Spent evening in writing to P.J.Z. & studying.

———

Commenced to read the Epistle of James in the original.

$$\mathcal{Z}$$

January, Sunday 29. 1888.

Arose at 7 A.M. Read & held prayer-meeting in my room with some of the Grammar-School boys. Attended Service in 4th Ref. Ch. with — Mr. Phelps. Sang in choir. Subject "Anchor of the Soul" — Dr. Campbell Attended S.S. in P.M.

Translated Dutch letter for Dr. Drury.[39]

Heard Sermon in P.M. by Dr. Campbell on "The Pharisee & Publican." Very eloquent effort. No Prayer Meeting. Read Bible & Müllers[40] life v [of] Trust in Evening. F.S. Scudder made me a call.

$$\mathcal{Z}$$

36 Graham Taylor (1851-1938), New Brunswick Theological Seminary, 1873. DD, Rutgers College, 1888. HD, 387

37 Maud Zwemer (1851-1928), sister of Samuel Zwemer.

38 William Pierson Merrill (1867-1954), UTS, 1890. UTS, 138

39 John Benjamin Drury (1838-1909), Editor, *Christian Intelligencer*, 1887-1909. HD, 112

40 George Müller (1805-1898), Evangelist and Missionary.

January, Monday 30. 1888.

Attended Recitations in A.M. Dr. Woodbridge gave a lecture on Proverbs. & its relations to the rest of the Bible. Very Valuable book to learn by heart. Read & studied in P.M. Wrote letters. Exercised in the Gymnasium. Read Greek with Rev. Willis (Jas 2.)

Spent evening in my room.

Received a letter from my sister Maud.

§

January, Tuesday 31. 1888.

Arose at 7.00 A.M. Read & Studied. Attended Recitations. Sermon by Mr. Furbeck[41]. Very good language but not practical; too much oratory & not enough "home-thrust" Studied in the P.M.

Read Medicine one hour. Exercised in the Gymnasium. Led Meeting of the Mission Band.

Subject "the South Sea Islands." Very pleasant meeting. Attended 4th Ref. Ch. Prayer Meeting. Dr. Mabon led. Was invited to take a sleigh-ride to-morrow night, with a party of young people.

Walked home with Mr. Phelps. Read Bible. Wrote letter to Miss. Kollen Retired at 12 P.M.

---

[41]   George Warren Furbeck (1864-1926), New Brunswick Theological Seminary, 1890. HD, 142

February 1888

February, Wednesday 1. 1888.

Attended Recitations. Dr. Lansing in Exegesis of Gen 1:1-4.

Dr. Woodbridge lecture on Ecclesiastes & Song of Solomon. "Text of the preacher is "Vanity. of Van. all is vanity". <u>Nature</u> is one endless circuit; all the <u>pleasures</u> of life are vanity; <u>wisdom</u> is vanity. Enjoy God's Blessings & be thankful. Remember Judgement!"

Attended Prayer Meeting.

Studied Lessons. Exercised in the Gymnasium. Read Greek. Went to home of Miss Demarest to meet a party of young people & go on a sleigh-ride. Fine weather; good sleighing. Drive to Metuchen. Met Rev. & Mrs. Wÿkhof[1] very pleasant people at the home of Westervelt where we had dinner. Very pleasant evening.

Enjoyed myself very much. Retired at 2.30 a.m.

> ♀

February, Thursday 2. 1888.

Arose at 7 A.M. Attended Recitations. Recd. letter from Alexandria Seminary in relation to the Missy Conference in Feb. 1888.

Studied & Read Bible in P.M. Went to South River for Mr. Duncombe[2] to lead a gospel service. Drove down there with Mr. Hugh. A pleasant ride of six miles. Meeting in the Baptist Church; about 40 present. Took for my subject John 4:10.

Spoke about 30 minutes. Spoke to an inquirers. Drive home very pleasant good sleighing but quite cold.

Retired at 12 M.

Recd. Postal from Union Sem. as to the Conference in Feb.

More than $700 already raised for our own Missionary.

> ♀

February, Friday 3. 1888.

Attended Recitations.

Heard some very pointed remarks by Dr. Woodbridge against "Episcopalianism".

Read essay on "The Connect" between the Old & the New Testaments".

[1] Garrett Wyckoff (1855-1921), Pastor, First Reformed Church, Metuchen, NJ. 1887-1894 HD, 475
[2] Alfred Duncombe (1861-1944), Rutgers College, 1893. HD, 114

Studied & Read in P.M. Prepared Prayer Meeting talk. Read Greek.
Led Cottage Prayer-Meeting at Throop Ave.
Subject Is.12
Retired early. Wrote letter to Henrietta Zwemer[3].
Received letter from A.B.R. to-day. A fine letter!

February, Saturday 4. 1888.

Studied. Read.
Commenced to write a sermon on John 8:12. Wrote six pages this
A.M. Mended clothing; oh what a poor hand I am at sewing!
Exercised in the Gymnasium. Sent for pair of pantaloons to
the Plymouth Rock Pants Co. of Boston Mass. $3.40. Attended choir-
meeting at Dr. Mabons.
Read Bible. 130th Psalm is worthy of study. The De Profundis,
Gloria in Excelsis Psalm.
Took Bath as usual & retired.

February, Sunday 5. 1888.

Held a morning prayer-meeting in my room. Attended services in
the 4th Ref. Ch. Dr. Drury preached on Gen 4:9
Very good language but poor delivery. He reads his sermons
entirely. Went to service in the County Jail with Mr. Duncombe. Visited
several families on Throop Ave.
Met Mrs. — a lady in the last stages of consumption. She was
resigned & ready to die. Got my feet wet through & through walking
through the common.
Took supper at the Hall. Evening Prayers were a blessing. Spent
Evening in Reading Bible. Life of Trust by Müller & Dream Life by Ike
Marvel[4]. Both these books are very fine.
Enjoyed a season of prayer.

---

[3]   Henrietta Zwemer (1864-1942), sister of Samuel Zwemer.
[4]   Donald Grant Mitchell (1822-1908), wrote under the pen name Ik Marvel.

February, Monday 6. 1888.

George Müllers life of Trust makes one feel the power of prayer. Why can we not all live in that way? Much prayer brings us near to God. Last night in the Evening Meeting Mr. D. said that the first & last words of Xt. were "My fathers business" — "uttermost parts v [of] 1 [the] earth." Blessed thought.

Attended Recitations. Wrote & at Sermon this A.M.

Read I & II Kings in Bible. Studied & wrote sermon in evening. Have a bad cold in my head. New Jersey climate is not healthy. Too warm in winter.

§

February, Tuesday 7. 1888.

Shipped Crayon Drawing of Mother home. Packed it as securely as possible. I hope it will get home safe & in time for Fathers birthday on the 12th inst..

Did not attend Recitations. Read Medicine & wrote letter to A.B. Reed.

Attended meeting of Mission Circle. John Allen read paper on Sandwich Islands. Com. were appointed to inform speakers & provide entertainment for delegates. Wrote letters to Dr. A.T. Pierson[5] J.W. Gaven, Cobb & Ferris. Sent latter $12.00 for Foreign Missions.

Read Bible & Retired.

Enjoyed a season of prayer. Received a direct answer to prayer as shown by a postal I received from P.J.Z.

§

February, Wednesday 8. 1888.

Arose at 7.00 A.M. Attended Recitations. & Prayer Meeting at noon. Studied. Called on Pres. Gates[6] & Dr. Doolittle[7]. Enquired at Printers as to the price of programs for the Alliance.

---

[5] Arthur Tappan Pierson (1837-1911), Editor, *Missionary Review of the World.* 1888-1911

[6] Merrill Edwards Gates (1848-1922), President, Rutgers College, 1882-1890. Rutgers, 45

[7] Theodore Sandford Doolittle (1836-1893), Professor, Rutgers College, 1864-1893. HD, 109

Edgar Tilton Jr.

Attended Meet v [of] 1 [the] Soc v [of] Inquiry. Acted as Secty. The appointments were made for speakers to deliver the final sermon at the end of the year before our Society.

Read II Chronicles, studied Hebrew & received a call from Mr. Tilton[8].

$$\mathcal{Z}$$

February, Thursday 9. 1888.

[No Entry]

$$\mathcal{Z}$$

February, Friday 10. 1888.

Bishop Coxe[9] lectured for the Society of Inquiry this A.M. He is an old man but a pleasing & lively speaker. He spoke on the Crisis of our country & the need of a greater cooperation of forces. Went to Dr. Applegate with Mr. Duncombe. Recd. Prescription for my cold. Went to Cottage Prayer-Meeting. Saw one soul brought into the kingdom. Partly through my instrumentality. Glory be to Him alone.

[8]   Edgar Tilton Jr. (1865-1954), New Brunswick Theological Seminary, 1889. Raven, 159
[9]   Arthur Cleveland Coxe (1818-1896), Bishop of New York,1865-96.

Walked Home with Duncombe & had a com. Meeting in Cantines[10] Room.

Retired tired at 12 Midnight.

§

February, Saturday 11. 1888.

Spent A.M. in reading & in writing sermon.

Read a little. Wrote letters. Spent P.M. in Gymnasium & in Writing.

Attended Choir meeting & Read Bible in evening.

How beautifully the history of Mephiboseth is a type of sinner received by his king.

Read Acts etc. Retired. Recd. Letter to-day from S. Joldersma.[11]

§

February, Sunday 12. 1888.

Attended Service in A.M. Sermon By Dr. Campbell. For Outline see Sermon Outline Book. Attended S.S. In P.M. "Christ & 1 [the] little Ones". Had seven in my class. Attended Meety v [of] Visitors & Suptendents v [of] City Alliance in Y.M.C.A. Hall. About 400 present very interesty & businesslike Address by Pres. Gates, on the work. My Supt. is Dr. English & I am expected to visit about ten houses every month.

Attended Y.M.C.A. Meety. Went to Grammar School Prayer Meeting. Very good. Went to Throop Ave. Mission & spoke on Mephibosheth & David. Several promised to accept xt & to pray for guidance etc.

Thank God......

§

February, Monday 13. 1888.

Recd. Letter from Dr. A.T. Pierson of Philadelphia & Dr. Cobb v [of] New York relative to the Alliance. Read.. Attended Recita's Spent evening in writy at sermon.

---

[10] James Cantine (1861-1940), New Brunswick Theological Seminary, 1889. HD, 63
[11] Sije Joldersma (1856-1930), Samuel Zwemer's brother-in-law, married to Christina Zwemer (1860-1951).

Recd letter from Sye. Jol. & others.
Read Book of Acts.

♎

February, Tuesday 14. 1888.

Attended Recitations.
Dr. Mabon spoke on Orthodoxy & Heterodoxy & advocated Church Cooperation. Studied & Read in P.M. Wrote letters.
Recd. letter from A.B.R. Attended Meeting v [of] 1 [the] Mission Band. Resolved to hold three sessions of the Alliance. Was appointed on Program committee.
Spent evening in reading Bible & an address by Dr. Lansing. Retired at 11.30 P.M.

♎

February, Wednesday 15. 1888.

Attended Recitations
Read & Studied.
Read Medicine one hour. Called on Dr. Lansing relative to the Alliance. Wrote to P.J.Z. etc.
Had a pleasant season of prayer at the noon hour. Read in Evening & Retired after taking exercise with Indian Clubs.
My Bible reading today was in Isaiah. His profecies are fine & instructive. Oh that I might be touched with a coal from the altar. & be able to speak the gospel with power.

♎

February, Thursday 16. 1888.

Arose at 7.00 Read Attended Recitations. Read Essay on the Paschal Controversy between John & the Synoptics before Dr. DeWitt.
Had a blessed season of prayer with Mr. Duncombe. Studied. Read a little. Extemporized before Prof. Peabody.
Went to Dr. Campbells for dinner. Had a very pleasant time. The Old Doctor is full of life & told us some good stories about his early life. He is an example of xtian activity & devotions.
Saw some fine photographs of European Works of Art. Among others about 20 of the Madonna & Jesus. Went home at 9 P.M.
Read Bible & Retired.

John De Witt

♎

February, Friday 17. 1888.

[No Entry]

♎

February, Saturday 18. 1888.

Worked for arranging District Alliance.

Wrote 22 letters etc. Answered A.B.R.

February, Sunday 19. 1888.

Arose at 7.00 Read Bible. Attended Prayer Meeting in Phelps Room.

Attended service in Suydam Ref. Church. Dr. Demarest (see Sermon Sketches)

Attended S.S.; 7 in my class. Church service in P.M.

Dr. Demarest. "Trust in God" Led meeting of Xtian Workers & was appointed chairman. Remained at home in evening & read Miss'y Review.

Had a blessed day.

All days are blessed which are spent in His service. "Oh for a closer walk". Had a talk with Sharpley on a Domestic Miss'y meeting on March 1st 88. in our church. Hope to carry it out.

9

February, Monday 20. 1888.

Attended Recitations in A.M. Read. Wrote at sermon. Heard lecture in evening by Dr. C. Meyer on "the Image v [of] God" in which he endeavored to explain the account v [of] mans creation. Very logical & deep. His accent is pleasingly German. For full outline of argument see Book of Lectures. Wrote letters. Heard some cutting remarks by Dr. Mabon in regard to the Alliance being held without his permission.

Bought book on Comparitive Religions by J.F. Clarke[12]. Read & Retired.

9

February, Tuesday 21. 1888.

Attended Recitations. Attended Meetng of Mission Circle & helped arrange for the Alliance. Called on Dr. Hart[13] & Dr. Drury.

Attended 4th Ref. Ch.

Prayer Meeting in evening Dr. Campbell on 1 Phil:6. Walked Home with Mrs. Mabon; was asked to call in & did so. Had a piece of Apple-pie.

Dr. Mabon remarked that I appeared to be a pietist

Had a pleasant ½ hour v [of] conversation.
Wrote at sermon & retired.

9

February Wednesday 22. 1888.

Washington's Birthday — but Recitations all day. Attended them as usual. The Museum of the Seminary was formally opened at 230 this P.M. Addresses by Dr. Lansing, Judge Bookstaver[14] & Dr. Woodbridge. Several valuable additions were made & now for 1 first time shown: Mummy, statuary, tapestry, paintings, photographs etc. Arab tent Coins, idols, weapons etc. etc.

---

[12] James Freeman Clarke (1810-1888), Theologian, Unitarian minister, Author. *Britanica* 15th Ed. v3, 353

[13] Charles Edward Hart (1838-1916), Professor, Rutgers College, 1880-1907. HD, 164

[14] Henry Weller Bookstaver (1834-1907), Trustee, Rutgers College 1876-1907, Judge, Court of Common Pleas, NY 1885-1895. Rutgers, 126

Spent evening in study & finished sermon.

Arranged for a prayer-meeting in behalf of the Alliance for to-morrow at noon.

Retired at 12 P.M.

$$\mathcal{G}$$

February, Thursday 23. 1888.

Attended Recitations.

Read & Prepared for the coming alliance.

Met Mr. Wilder at the train. Supper at the Hall. Meeting at College Chapel in evening. Students Missionary Organization formed. Doolittle Pres. Phelps Secty. & Lansing Treasurer.

Heard a fine Missionary talk by Mr. Wilder.

Comparison of Home with Foreign fields.

Mr. Stoop[15] of Union slept in my room this evening & I slept on the floor in Mr. Sperlings[16] room. Expect a glorious time to-morrow.

$$\mathcal{G}$$

Dist. Missy. Alliance
February, Friday 24. 1888.

Arose at 6.30. Hung Miss'y maps in Chapel & took breakfast. Prepared Committee Room for reception of delegates. 60 were present. Morning session Hertzog Hall. Woodbridge Miyaki & reports. P.M. College Chapel – Sagebeer. Taylor, Wallace, Moyer & Wilder. – Grand papers. Evening. Gowen – "Lavers from Looking-glasses. Scudder L.R.[17] Medical Missions & Dr. A.T. Pierson – address on consecration & giving. After Meeting best of all. Holy Spirit present. Is. 6:8 was the expression of all. Took Dr. Pierson to the train & a grand worker he is.

A photograph of the Alliance was taken at 12 Mid-noon. Very pleasant day — some new volunteers. Held a praise service in Phelps room in evening.

$$\mathcal{G}$$

[15] James Porter Stoops (1862-1950), Union Seminary, 1890. UTS, 142
[16] Isaac Sperling (1860-1917), Rutgers College, 1890. HD, 370
[17] Lewis Rousseau Scudder (1861-1935), Missionary to India, 1888-1935. HD, 353

February, Saturday 25. 1888.

Rested out from toil.
Read & Wrote letters in A.M.
Reported the Alliance for the Christian Intelligencer.
Choir Meeting in evening. Very tired & headache.

𝕾

February, Sunday 26. 1888.

Bright Sabbath morning.
Prayer-meeting in my room. About 7 were present. Mr. Yoshida gave some good news from Japan. Attended Service in Suydam St. Church. — Dr. Mabon. — see Sermon Sketches. Very good delivery. Attended S.S. Had a pleasant time with my little girls.

Attended church. Dr. Campbell – on the Christian Home. Led Prayer Meeting: Xtian Boldness. Good Meeting. After supper Prayer meeting at the Hall. Went to Throop Ave. Mission Led the meeting. Mr. Yoshida spoke on Japan.

Spoke to an enquirer.
Spent remainder of day in reading Bible.

Blessed day of Restful Work

𝕾

February, Monday 27. 1888.

Attended Recitations.
Studied & Read in evening.

Wrote letters to Father. Maud etc.
Sent sermon to A.B.R.

𝕾

February, Tuesday 28. 1888.

Attended Recitations.
Made my calls as City Visitor in P.M. Called on nine families. 2 of them did not attend church. Saw much poverty & dirt. Read Bible in evening & prepared Envelope Scrap-Book. Sent Report to my Supervisor.

Read George Ebers[18] Bride v [of] 1 [the] Nile – A fascinating story of Egypt in the time v [of] 1 [the] Mukaukas & the Jacobite Controversy.

No Mission Meeting to-day.

$$\mathcal{G}$$

February, Wednesday 29. 1888.

Attended Recitations. Lecture on O. Test. Connection. Exegesis by Dr. Lansing.

No Prayer-Meeting to-day Read & Studied in P.M. Wrote letter to P.J.Z. & to Y.M.C.A. At Paterson.

Started article for "De-Hope" on Missions.

Read Greek with Rev. Willis. Attended Meeting v [of] Society v [of] Inquiry. Debated on question as to sanctity v [of] 1 [the] church-building as such. Read Zechariah & retired at 12 M.

Very busy day.

Answered father's letter & also Maud Z.

Heard some good results of the Alliance. At New York Med. Missy Institute. "Despise not the day of small things.

---

[18]   Georg Ebers (1837-1898), Egyptologist and Author.

March1888

March, Thursday 1. 1888.

Arose at 7 a.m. attended Recitations. Recd. letter from Mrs. Paulls. Pleasant to hear from old friends.

Read in P.M. called on Rev. Maddock M.E. Pastor in reference to City Mission Work. Started to make a Bible—Commonplace or Side-Light book. Wrote article for "De Hope" on Missions in Mexico. Attended lecture in Evening by Rev. Hermpstone of Calvary Baptist Church at Brooklyn on Darwin-Life & Letters [For outline see Back of book- "Origin of Species"] He is a very pleasing speaker but smiles incessantly. His manner was good. Read & Studied in evening. Had a discussion with Mr. Andrew until 12 M. on infant-salvation & <u>elect</u>ion.

$$\mathcal{Z}$$

March, Friday 2. 1888.

Attended Recitations. Studied. Wrote Article for de Hope & Made some entries in my Bible Commonplace book. Attended Cottage-Prayer. Meeting in evening. Very Pleasant meeting. Spoke on Ps. 130th.

Read in Evening.

$$\mathcal{Z}$$

March, Saturday 3. 1888.

Spent A.M. in study & in writing an outline of talk on Domestic Missy. work of our church.

Drew map of our frontier & sketches of 1st Ref. Church Le Mars Iowa & Academy v [of] 1 [the] North West. Called on Rev. J.T. Demarest[1] & need some books for the library v [of] 1 [the] Academy.

Spent evening at Choir rehearsal & in reading etc.

Pleasant weather to-day. Wrote letters to Miss. Kollen & others.

$$\mathcal{Z}$$

March, Sunday 4. 1888.

Attended Prayer Meeting in one of the students rooms. Attended service in Suydam Ref. Ch. Communion Services. Text. "All things ready come to the feast. Attended S.S. in P.M. [Attended] Church meeting & spoke on Domestic Missions on the Frontier.

---

[1]   John Terhune Demarest (1813-1897), Retired 1885. HD, 97

Took Supper. Attended evening prayers. It is nearly 4 years ago to-day that I joined church. How fast time flies. 4 years old! How much & yet how little I have grown- I can not walk alone even & have only just learned to talk for Him. Had a pleasant meeting at the 1st Ref. Ch. & an address on Foreign Miss. By Rev. Pockman[2]

$$\mathcal{Z}$$

March, Monday 5. 1888.

Recd. letter & returned Sermon from A.B.R. What queer mortals girls are!!!

Attended Recitations & Read Jeremiah in Bible. Spent P.M. in arranging Bible Index & indexing S.S. Times.

Recieved Telegram from P.J.Z. at Holland telling that they had raised $250. to aid us in sending out a foreign missionary. What a glorious answer to my prayers! Brother Duncombe called in the evening & we had a pleasant conversation. Wrote to Sister Nellie[2]. R.P. Wilder and others.

Retired at 1 A.M.

$$\mathcal{Z}$$

March, Tuesday 6. 1888.

Attended Recitations.

Studied. Called on Dr. J.T. Demarest & received a donation of some books to the North Western Class. Acad. Carried them in a satchel & a large package to my room.

Attended Meeeting of Mission Band.

Attended Prayer Meeting in evening at Suydam Ref. Ch. Dr. Campbell on Phil. 3:11.

Very interesting. Received a letter from Wilder etc.

Worked at Index in evening.

$$\mathcal{Z}$$

March, Wednesday 7. 1888.

Attended Recitations. In exegesis Dr. Lansing favored the idea that God had a body & drew his conclusions from Genesis 1. The question is worth investigating further.

[2]   Nellie Zwemer (1862-1945), sister of Samuel Zwemer.

William Henry Campbell

Attended prayer-meeting v [of] the students. Subject: Child training.

Studied & Read. Took a walk. Bound volume of Homiletic Monthlies.

Read & Wrote at correcting my first sermon in evening.

Recd. letter from Brother Albert & sister Kate[3]. & also from A.J.Z. In regard to foreign Missionary.

Read part of Jeremiah & retired at 12 P.M.

♀

March, Thursday 8. 1888.

Attended Recitations. Dr. De Witt promised me/some money to help me along. Read & packed books for the North Western Academy in P.M. Mr. Panling[4] is quite sick. Read Greek with Rev. Willis our rector. Attended Meeting of Missy. Society of the students of New Brunswick in evening. A great deal of discussion as to whom we shall send out for our money. Two ideas most prominent: Chamberlain to be supported or 7 new native-helpers. The meeting ended peaceably. Called on James Mabon[5] & borrowed V. dollars from him to help me out of a difficulty.

---

[3]   Catharina Adriana Strabbing (nee Zwemer) (1859-1944), sister of Samuel Zwemer.
[4]   Likely Henry Wemple Pawling (1868-1903), Rutgers College, 1892. Rutgers, 211
[5]   James Mabon (1866-1941), son of William Van Vranken Mabon.

Remained up until 3 A.M. With Mr. Panling who is quite sick.

§

March, Friday 9. 1888.

Attended Recitations.
Read & Studied in P.M.
Recd. 20$ from Dr. De Witt to-day in answer to my prayer for temporal needs. Bought a shirt & 3 pair socks etc
Read Greek with Rev. Willis — commenced to read book of Revelation.

Attended Young People's Union of Suydam St. Ref. Church. Had a spelling match.

Walked home & read Spurgeons lectures for a short time.
Retired at 10 P.M.

§

March, Saturday 10. 1888.

Arose late this A.M. & Missed my breakfast. Studied & Read.

Wrote essay on "Moravian Mission Work." for the Society of Inquiry
Very interesting subject How much these willing consecrated workers are doing & have done for xt.

Took a four miles walk with F.S. Scudder in P.M. over the long bridge & the tow-path of the Raritan River.
Spent evening in writing to A.B.R. & study.

§

March, Sunday 11. 1888.

Attended Morning Prayer-Meeting in Mr. Phelp's Room. Went to Ger. Ref. Church & heard Rev. Dr. Meyer[6] on Daniel 4:34 "PAulz"
Very powerful in delivery. Attended Suydam St. S.S.

& Meeting of Y.M.C.A. After supper went to the home of Rev. Stugres - & went with him to the colored M.E. Church.

[6]   Carl Meyer (1824-1901), Pastor, Third, New Brunswick, NJ, 1869-1901, Professor, Rutgers College, 1869-1901. HD, 266

Preached for the first time Was helped & blessed in answer to my prayers. Text Jno. 4:10.

Not a very large but an attentive audience. Very rainy & cold. Enjoyed myself to-day. Read the latter part of Jeremiah and then Retired at 10.30 P.M.

$$\mathcal{Z}$$

March, Monday 12. 1888.

Arose at 6 A.M. <u>Heavy</u> Blizzard[7] – worse than they have seen here for years.

Helped the Milk-man out of the snow.

Spent day in the house. All trains stopped. No Mail. Wrote article for "Mission-Field & answered letters. Read Bible in evening and worked & read for Missionary Essay.

Very cold this evening. At 11:30 I witnessed a remarkable electric display Balls of fire-green and red were seen over the city and lightning incessant without thunder. The storm still continues.

$$\mathcal{Z}$$

March, Tuesday 13. 1888.

Arose at 7 A.M. Remained at my room. Storm still continues. No Mail.

Studied & Read.

Went up town in P.M. and had photograph taken of 5 of the boys standing in a snow-drift. Very cold and disagreeable.

Read Greek with Rev. Willis. Called on Mrs. Mabon in evening. Met Mr. & Mrs. Mabon Jr. nice people.

All the Profs. Seem to have been caught in the storm & we have no recitations.

$$\mathcal{Z}$$

March, Wednesday 14. 1888.

Still Vacation. Storm has ceased but the roads are in a fearful condition & no mail has yet been received.

---

[7] The Great Blizzard of 1888 also referred to as the Great White Hurricane, March 11-14, 1888. https://www.britannica.com/event/Great-Blizzard-of-1888.

Read & Studied.

Took walk to Wreck near Metuchen. 4 Locomotives off the rails and badly injured.

More than 200 men digging for the R.R. Co.

Bought a pair of Rubber-boots to weather the storm. Wrote letters in evening.

March, Thursday 15. 1888.

Trains are beginning to come in. First mail for four days this A.M. Read & Studied for Sermon in Dutch & Prize essay in English. Took clock to repairer. Some of the boys returned from New York to-day & said that the city suffered a great deal in the storm. — the most severe for more than 30 years. To me it did not appear much worse than a regular snow-storm in Michigan — such as we had every winter more than once.

Read letters from home! Read. Wrote at Sermon & Retired After reading Bible. At 10:30.

March, Friday 16. 1888.

Attended Recitations except Lansing
Read Gospel of John. Studied on Dutch Sermon & wrote letters.
Recd. letter from Jno. Lamar.
Have a bad cold & do not feel very bright & strong.

March, Saturday 17. 1888.

Arose at 7.30. Breakfast. Spent morning in reading on Missions & studying & writing an address on Missions for Princeton next Sunday (25th.) Subject: Opportunities.

Read Romans. Fine thought & accurate logic! No book like the Bible! Read & Patched clothing in P.M. Read Greek with Rev. Willis.

Attended choir-meeting. Weather pleasant & quite warm.

Recd. letter from brother P.J.Z. to-day he is making a grand success of his studies this year.

Wrote & Retired after taking a bath at 10:30.

George Warren Furbeck

March, Sunday 18. 1888.

Arose at 7 A.M. Attended Prayer Meeting in Furbeck's Room after breakfast. Went to Suydam St. Ref. Ch. Sermon by Rev. Campbell Heb. 12:6. Very interesting.

Attended S.S. in P.M. taught a Missionary lesson. They were much interested & promised to give all they could every week. Attended church-service. Led Prayer Meeting after Service: "What shall I do with my life?"

Good meeting. Made a call on Dr. Campbell & took supper at Dr. Mabon's. —

Pleasant time.

Spoke on For. Missions at Throop Avenue. About 75 present & all much interested. Mr. Duncombe spoke on Missions also. Walked home with Dun. What a blessed day this has been.

March, Monday 19. 1888.

Arose late. Headache. Attended Recitations. Went to Doctor for Mr. Furbeck who feels quite sick.

Read & Studied in evening Finished Article for the Press.

Went to various city papers & had an appeal to the churches in behalf of Foreign Missions published in accordance with a request from R.P. Wilder.

Retired at 11.30 P.M.

§

March, Tuesday 20. 1888.

Arose at 7.30. Attended Recitation except Dr. G.J. [J.G.] Lansing who was absent.

Read Psalms 100-130. Studied in P.M. & met Rev. Poole [Pool][8] the Home Missy secty. of our Denomination & applied for work this summer.

Wrote to Dr. A.T. Pierson about attending the London World Conference for Missions. Hope God will open the way that many may go.

Attended Prayer meeting walked home with Miss. Garner.

Pleasant weather today although wet in the A.M.

Retired at 11 P.M.

§

March, Wednesday 21. 1888.

Arose at 630 A.M. Attended Recitations & meeting of Seminary Students. No Prayer meeting. Studied & arranged for a prayer-meeting in behalf for Peace at the Missy meeting this evening. I feared we would have trouble as Pres. Gates was strongly in favor of Rev. Chamberlain[9] as our Miss. & the Seminary men for a new man in the field.

Good Prayer Meeting at 6.30 Election of Missionary at 7.00 God heard our prayers; after a very hot discussion during which Dr. Lansing & Mabon withdrew, there was a unanimous vote in favor of sending out & supporting Rev. L.R. Scudder M.D. to India. Held Praise meetings in Furbecks room & in my room with Mr. Duncombe. Received letter from A.T. Pierson.

§

---

[8]   Charles Hubbard Pool (1840-1906), Secretary, Board of Domestic Missions, 1887-1906. HD, 311

[9]   Could be referring to William Isaac Chamberlain (1862-1937), Missionary to India 1887-1905. or Jacob Chamberlain (1835-1908), Missionary to India 1859-1908. HD, 65

March, Thursday 22. 1888.

Attended Recitations & Read & Studied in P.M. Commenced to Read Epistle to the Romans in Greek.

Wrote article for "De Hope" on Foreign Missions.

Meeting of Soc. V [of] Inquiry in evening.

9

March, Friday 23. 1888.

Attended Recitations.

Read some Dutch for Dr. Mabon. Spent P.M. in study etc.

Attended Social of Suydam St. Ref. Ch. in evening.

Called on Dr. Drury etc. Recd. a cake for present from Arthur Mabon.

Mabon boys called in evening. Retired at 12 M.

Subscribed 10¢ weekly for congregational expenses.

9

March, Saturday 24. 1888.

Read & Prepared speech for Princeton in A.M.

Hope I shall be aided in speaking to-morrow. Mr. Keeling[10] is going with me. Although I am sorry Phelps has changed his mind about going I hope we shall get along with two of us. Recd. letter this A.M. from Peeke in Japan. He seems to enjoy himself.

Took train at 3.14 for Priceton; changed at the Junction. Met at Depot by Mr. Fisk[11]. Saw Princeton College; Nassau Hall N.E. & VV College Museum. Library Chapel & Murray Hall. -fine set of buildings— Also Dr. McCosh's[12] Residence & grounds. Visited the Seminary After tea took a walk up to the Observatory & had a view of the moon through the Observatory Telescope. Grand.

9

[10] James Harvey Keeling (1864-?), Rutgers College, 1889. Rutgers, 201
[11] Charles Ezra Fisk (1863-?), Princeton Theological Seminary, 1886-88. PTS, 418
[12] James McCosh (1811-1894), President, Princeton University, 1868-1888, Professor, Princeton University, 1868-1894. 1911 *Britannica*, 206

Prayer-meeting in <u>Stuart Hall</u>.
March, Sunday 25. 1888.

Arose at 7.30. Breakfasted at the club with Mr. Dr. Fisk & Murray.[13] Went to Penn's Neck Baptist Church in A.M. quite good audience; spoke on Missions & succeeded in interesting them. Took dinner at Rev. Love. He & she are fine people; have a daughter f is a Volunteer at Peddie Inst.[14] — Hightstown N.J. Went to Chapel in P.M. heard an address by Rev. Poor Sect'y of Pres. Bd. Of Ed. To the point. Missy Meeting in parlors. Attended Missy meeting v [of] students at 7 P.M. & then walked to Stony Brook School-house & spoke on Missions. Succeeded in raising @ 3.00 in cash & in pleding 24.00 for support of a native teacher in Japan. <u>How God has blessed me this day</u>! Prayer-meeting in Mr. Towler's[15] Room.

Retired at 10:30.

℘

March, Monday 26. 1888.

Arose at 7.00 Took breakfast at the club & took a walk through the college-building & grounds. Took train at 9:38 A.M. for New Brunswick. Spent P.M. & evening in study & writing essay on Confucianism for Dr. Mabon.

Read Book of Daniel.

Retired at 11:30

℘

March, Tueday 27. 1888.

Arose at 700.

Attended Recitations & read essay.

Studied in P.M. Read book of Hosea. Attended meeting of Mission Circle. Was appointed a com. to see to the procuring of a room for our meetings & the publication of Missionary Pamphlet. Read <u>Vondel's</u>[16] Lucifer in evening & studied & wrote at Dutch Sermon.

℘

13   David Ambrose Murray (1861-?), Princeton Theological Seminary, 1888. PTS, 419
14   Peddie Institute, founded 1864 as a Baptist preparatory school.https://www.peddie. org/about-us/history-traditions
15   Lewis Howell Towler (1860-1899), Princeton Theological Seminary 1888. PTS, 428
16   Joost van den Vondel (1587-1679), Poet, Playwright. https://en.wikipedia.org/wiki/ Joost_van_den_Vondel

March, Wednesday 28. 1888.

Attended Recitations.

Read paper before Soc. V [of] Inquiry on Moravian Missy. Work.

$$\wr$$

March, Tuesday 29. 1888.

Attended Recitations.

Took train at 2:20 P.M. for New York City. With Mr. Talmadge [Talmage][17].

Saw streets etc. Trinity Cathedral. Ascended Mutual Insurance Buildy. Took supper at Restaurant & went to Inter. Med. Miss. Assoc. in evening. Pleasant hour of prayer with the students & talk with Rev. L.R. Scudder our Missionary elect.

Remained at the Grand Union Hotel overnight. Fine equipment & reasonable rates.

Retired late.

Pleasant day.

$$\wr$$

March, Friday 30. 1888.

Arose at 7.00 Breakfast at a Restaurant. Madison Ave cars to 69th St. Union Theological Seminary. Met Mr. Wilder & Stoops. Pleasant conversation on Volunteers & the London World Conference. Spoke with Stoops on going to Chester Pa. to speak on Missions.

Cars 3rd ave. Saw Battery & Castle Garden & ascended the Washington Building. 262 ft. high.

Saw U.S. Assay office; delicate scales. Bars of gold $40,000.00 Called at Pres. Bd. For. Missions. Took Ferry to Jersey City & returned home.

Choir meeting in evening. Pleasant time.

$$\wr$$

---

[17]   George Edwin Talmage (1865-1944), New Brunswick Theological Seminary, 1890. HD, 385

March, Saturday 31. 1888.

Studied & Read. Arranged for meeting on Sun. 8th April in Meth. E. Church for delegation from Princeton. Read <u>Amos</u> & <u>Obadiah</u>. How finely the style of Amos agrees with the <u>man</u>.

Read & Studied in P.M. Attended choir meeting in evening & helped decorate the church for easter. One way of keeping Easter it seems is to have Fine flowers & fine music!! Where does the <u>service</u> come in?

Is it serving God to sing-songs about him or to string up roses & lilies? These things can do no harm if d<u>one</u> but we should not leave the other u<u>ndone</u>.

April 1888

April, Sunday 1. 1888.

Prayer-meeting in my Room. Attended Service in Suydam St. Ref. Ch. Good Sermon on text: "He is not here; he is risen." Sang 1st Bass in choir.

Attended S.S. in P.M. My class began to contribute to Missions 39¢ in one week! Pleasant hour.

Attended Church. Rev. Willis' delivered a sermon. Young Peoples prayer-meeting Very good. "Xtian armour." Supper at the Hall.

Prayer Meeting at the Hall.

Went to Throop-ave. in evening & spoke on the Resurrection. Pleasant walk home with Mr. Duncombe.

This has been a day of blessing for me.

Francis R. Havergal[1] used to write "Daily Mercies" in her Journal:— I think it a good plan

April, Monday 2. 1888.

Arose at 7.00 attended Recitations. Wrote article for "Missy. Review of the World" on our Mission Band I work.

Pleasant weather. Spring & the grind-organ have come!

Read Bible at noon.

Spent evening in letter-writing & study.

Recd. letter from brother Peter saying that he joined church last Sabbath. Good.

Retired at 11.30 after exercise with Indian Clubs as usual.

April, Tuesday 3. 1888.

Attended Recitations.

Sent article on India to "De Hope"

Read & Studied. Mission Circle met in Phelp's Room.

April, Wednesday 4. 1888.

Attended Recitations as usual.

[1] Francis R. Havergal (1836-1879), Poet. en.wikipedia.org/wiki/Frances_Ridley_Havergal

Samuel Merrill Woodbridge

April, Thursday 5. 1888.

Attended Recitations.

Studied in P.M.

Dr. J.S. Mac Arthur of New York lectured for us on Expository Preaching this evening. Very good & interesting speaker. He advised the more through study v [of] 1 [the] original text. Went to teachers meeting through the rain.

First heavy shower and first thunder shower this year. Weather fine to-day.

April, Friday 6. 1888.

Attended Recitations as usual.

Essay for Dr. Mabon on Buddhism etc.

First recitation in Arabic to-day. Found it very pleasant & interesting. Am in great doubts what best to do this summer! I hope an "open door" will be set before me.

Took dinner at Dr. S.M. Woodbridge this evening. Very pleasant time. Dr. W. has a large family & a happy one it seems. Retired at 11:30.

♫

April, Saturday 7. 1888.

Studied and Read in A.M. Wrote letter to H.V.S. Peeke in Japan.

In afternoon Mr. Jim Mabon asked me to go out for a drive; we went five miles into the country & visited Little Washington. Very pleasant weather & altogether a delightful drive. Mabon Family have treated me like a lord their hospitality & kindness is unbounded.

Spent evening in entertaining the delegates from Princeton — Mr. Towler[2] and Eckels[3] who come here to speak on Foreign Missions.

Very pleasant fellows & consecrated to the work.

♫

April, Sunday 8. 1888.

Arose at 7:00. Read Bible & took breakfast at the Hall with the Princeton fellows. Attended 4th Ref. Church in A.M. & heard a grand sermon expository by Dr. Campbell on 1 Timothy 4:12. He has a wonderful power of language & a way of putting things.

Attended S.S. Class of 6. Lesson on Christ & the Pharisees. Spoke on "The Boundaries of Mission -work" in the church. Mr. Eckels spoke on Opportunity Mr. Yowler spoke on Duty. Supper at the hall.

Went to 1st M.E. Church in Evening. Made an address on Missions taking for my subject "Gas-jets, Pyramids & Fire". showing the benefits of Union v [of] work and of energy & push.

Retired at 11 P.M. after a short prayer-meeting.

♫

April, Monday 9. 1888.

Attended Recitations & Studied in P.M.

Spent evening in writing etc. Recd. letter from Princeton relative to trip to London in June.

---

[2] Lewis Howell Towler (1860-1899), Princeton Theological Seminary, 1889. PTS, 428
[3] Charles Edmund Eckels (1861-?), Princeton Theological Seminary, 1887-88. PTS, 417

༄

April, Tuesday 10. 1888.

Arose at 6.30 Attended Recitations. Spent P.M. in Study. Read an essay on Medical Mission before the Mission Band at 5 P.M.

After tea attended Arabic recitation at Dr. J.G. Lansing. Very pleasant & social evening. The Arabic has a peculiar vowel-system which is somewhat difficult to master.

Saw a fine collection v [of] coins belonging to Dr. Lansing. Some going as far back as Philip of Macedon & even further. The Chinese have round coins with a square hole in centre.

Most ancient coins are circular while the very earliest are of square shape.

༄

April, Wednesday 11. 1888.

Attended Recitations as usual. Took train at 12:55 for New York in company with John Allen. Visited the various Steam Ship lines to ascertain rates for Europe. Met Mr. Phelps & Boocock[4] at the Jersey City Depot & with them took the Brooklyn Annex for Brooklyn. Cars to Flatbush. Pleasant hour in preparing for Stereopticon Exhibition with Mr. Phelps in the chapel of Flatbush.

Dinner at Mrs. Gertrude Vander Bilt[5] — the author. Pleasant & social time. Delivered lecture: "Around the world in 80 minutes" Quite good audience.

Took cars across bridge & train at 10:30 home.

Retired at 12 M.

༄

April, Thursday 12. 1888.

Attended Recitations.

My birthday to-day! 21 years. How time has passed since I came East.

---

4   William Henry Boocock (1863-1928), Pastor, Grace Chapel, Flatbush, Brooklyn, 1888-99. Raven, 157

5   Gertrude Lefferts Vanderbilt (1824-1902), Author, *The Social History of Flatbush* (1881). https://www.findagrave.com/memorial/57305504/gertrude-vanderbilt; http://www.brownstonedetectives.com/tilting-at-the-flatbush-windmill-1879/

Oh may my life in the future be one of usefulness! Have prayed that God would consecrate me to the work for For. Missions. May my only motive be his honor and glory.

Oh how much we seek our own glory instead of His. Attended Lecture in chapel by Rev. R.R. Meredith[6] On Subject: "What & How to preach" Very interesting.

Wrote letter to Sister Henrietta[7] and retired early as I am very tired.

$$\wp$$

April, Friday 13. 1888.

Attended Recitations. Read essay on "Gods of Egypt" for Dr. Mabon.

Studied & took a long walk in P.M.

Attended Arabic Recita' in evening. Dr. Lansing is very kind & sociable.

He advised us to keep up a thourough knowledge v [of] 1 [the] Hebrew and arabic

After leaving the Seminary. Read. Wrote to Sister Mary & Retired at 10 P.M.

$$\wp$$

April, Saturday 14. 1888.

Arose at 6.30. Studied in A.M. Wrote letter to Mr. Lorenz[8] of Union Seminary to inform him of regard to The Missionary Movement at New Brunswick & 1 [the] support v [of]a College Missionary.

Took walk up town.

Spent P.M. in reading & study. Commenced to read Victor Hugo's[9] novel "Les Miserable" in French. Quite interesting. Took dinner at Dr. Demarest on invitation at 6:30. Met Mrs. D. and other worthies & had a good social time.

---

6 Likely Rev. Robert R. Meredith Pastor, Tompkins Avenue Congregational Church 1887-1902. www.nytimes.com/1902/06/09/archives/rev-dr-meredith-resigns-continued-illhealth-compels-him-to-give-up.html
7 Henrietta Zwemer (1864-1942), sister of Samuel Zwermer. See MH.
8 Daniel Edward Lorenz (1862-?), UTS, 1889. UTS, 133
9 Victor Hugo (1802-1885), Novelist. *Britannica* 15th Ed. v6, 125

Attended Choir-meeting at Mr. Willis.
Read & Retired at 11.30.

§

April, Sunday 15. 1888.

Arose at 6.30. Read Bible. After breakfast attended consecration-meeting in Mr. Duncombe's room.

Service in A.M. at Suydam St. Ref. Ch. Sermon on 1 Kings 18:21 by Dr. J.T. Demarest. Interesting but too "<u>funny</u>" for a gospel sermon.

Went to County-Jail in P.M. & led meeting for prisoners. 4 of them asked for prayers! Visited "the sick" with Alfred D. Attended a cottage-prayer meeting of the Salvation Army. They have done a grand work in their way. Supper at Mrs. Ruhs. Very hospitable & kind. Throop Ave. Mission in Eveeny. Spoke on "Xtian Work" —

"Son go work to-day in my vine<u>ya</u>rd.

Blessed-day & full of mercies & loving-kindness.

§

April, Monday 16. 1888.

Attended Recitations in A.M. Read Hebrew and studied. Recd. Registered package for my birthday—21 dimes from father & $5.00 from Sister Maud.

Helped Prof. Doolittle arrange screen for Stereoptican Exhibition.

Attended lecture (illustrated) by Rev. Ingersoll[10] on "the Ideal Christ in Art"

Very interesting. It is surprising how the nationality of the artist appears in his picture.

Retired after reading a while.

§

April, Tuesday 17. 1888.

Attended Recitations.

Essay on Mohammedism. Studied. Wrote letters to Hospers. F.J.Z. And Maud.

---

[10]   Could be refering to Edward Payson Ingersoll (1834-1907), Pastor, Puritan Congregational Church, 1882-91. HD, 192

Made a visit to Dr. English No Mission-Band meeting this afternoon. Recited Arabic in evening.

§

April, Wednesday 18. 1888.

Attended Recitations. Pleasant hour with Dr. Lansing in Exegesis. Attended Meeting of Society of Inquiry in Evening & heard a debate on the subject "Resolved & the need for workers at home is greater than in the Foreign field"! What a question for discussion! Attended first lecture of the "Vedder" Course by Dr. Cooper[11] on "Doubt: Irrational"

Very logical – but dry & not practical enough.

§

April, Thursday 19. 1888.

Attended Recitations & Recited Arabic (special) in evening.

Received letter to-day from brother Peter which was very interesting. Affairs at Hope seems to prosper.

§

April, Friday 20. 1888.

Attended Recitations as usual.

Brought coat to tailor for repairs.

Took train at 12.55 P.M. for New York. Saw Stock Exchange visited Jas. Mabon at Brown Brothers & company.

Went to Union Theol. Sem. & met Mr. Wilder again. What a grand fellow he is; his very face is an inspiration.

Took a view of the buildings. After tea went with Mr. Ford[12] to June St. M.E. Church & heard Harris the boy-preacher—Revival Services— Good. A few objectionable features however – but they [sp?] are of little account when we think of the souls saved. Slept at Union Th. Sem.

§

[11] Jacob Cooper (1830-1904), Vedder Lecturer, New Brunswick Theological Seminary, 1887-88. Raven, 44
[12] Lorraine Harold Forde (1863-1948), UTS, 1886-1889. UTS, 131

April, Saturday 21. 1888.

Took Elevated 3ʳᵈ Ave car to Bible House. Met Editor of Gospel in All Lands & Rev. McLean[13] D sl.

Bought a fountain-pen for the money I received from Mand & Nellie for my birthday. Took Christopher street ferry for Hoboken & thence a car for Union Hill — Wheehawken P. C. Where I am to visit Rev. I.W. Gowen[14] — editor of the Mission Field. Pleasant Reception. Good wife. Drive to Hackensack & a visit to Rev. VanderWart[15] in afternoon.

Spent evening in Conversation with Mr. & Mrs. Gowen both nice people.

Mrs. G. reads Greek etc. etc. & is quite a genious. She keeps Rev. G's papers in order etc. Wilbur & Hazel are destined for the Mission Field.

≈

April, Sunday 22. 1888.

After a pleasant night — rest in the old-parsonage arose at 6.30 A.M. Family Prayers.

Attended S.S. & taught a class v [of] girls on 1 [the] parable v [of] 1 [the] Ten Virgins. Heard Rev. Gowen preach in A.M. on 1 [the] last verse in 1 [the] Bible. Very good style v [of] preaching & popular in its character.

Attended Turnpike S.S. in P.M. taught class of boys. The Turnpike S.S. & chapel is @ a mile distant fr 1 [the] Grove Church. Supper at Rev. I.W.G. & at 7 P.M. a walk to Mission Church. Preached there in evening on John 8:12 Full house & mostly young people. Was a little nervous but was helped in preaching. Attended Young People's Meeting at 9 o'clock. Rev. G. spoke to-day concerning my work in the coming vacation. He wants an agent for the Mission Field. I think of accepting the work.

≈

April, Monday 23. 1888.

Arose at 7.00 Breakfast — a good one prepared by Mrs. Gowen! Rev. & Mrs. Accompanied me to 1 [the] Horse-car & thence I went to

---

13   Possibly Charles M. McLean
14   Isaac William Gowen (1858-1929), Pastor, Grove, North Bergen, NJ, 1885-1929. HD, 150
15   Herman Vanderwart (1852-1910), Pastor, First, Hackensack, NJ, 1886-1910. HD, 415

Barclay St. Ferry. Visit at Intelligencer Office & at 26 Reade St. where Rev. H.N. Cobb[16] spoke to me about giving Missionary Addresses at the various churches this year.

Made a visit to the Tombs & the Police Courts & took train at 1 P.M. for home. Read. wrote to Peter F. & studied.

Busy day but full of blessings. Called on Dr. Campbell on request. He Spoke to me about tutoring a son of Mr. C. Hardenberg[17]. Retired at 10.30

§

April, Tuesday 24. 1888.

Attended Recitations & read essay on the Standards for Dr. Mabon.

Studied. Dinner at Mr. Hardenberg - met my future pupil - what a case of total depravity! Only son — spoiled child. Studied Hebrew Arabic etc. Meeting of Mission Band — Farewell to Jno M. Allen. & pleasant hour of prayer. Spent evening in reciting Arabic & in writing an article on Missions for "De Hope".

Retired at 1 A.M.

§

Began to teach.
April, Wendesday 25. 1888.

Attended Recitations.

Good Prayer-meeting at noon. Mr. Garabed[18] spoke of God as a refuge in time of trouble. Made my first visit on Mr. Alex. Hardenberg[19] & assigned him lessons etc in the various branches.

Studied. Read Moffat's[20] life - what a grand history.

[16] Henry Nitchie Cobb (1834-1910), Secretary, Board of Foreign Missions, 1883-1910. HD, 71
[17] Cornelius Lowe Hardebergh (1834-1873), Real Estate Agent, father of Alexander Hardenbergh. www.myheritage.com/research/record-40001-282590448/cornelius-lowe-hardenbergh-in-familysearch-family-tree?s=542832841
[18] H. Garabed (1858-?), New Brunswick Theological Seminary, 1889. Raven, 159
[19] Alexander McClellan Hardenbergh (1873-?), son of C.L. Hardenbergh.www.myheritage.com/research/record-40001-197056166/alexander-mcclellan-hardenberg-in-familysearch-family-tree?s=542832841
[20] Robert Moffat (1795-1883), Missionary to Africa, biblical translator. *Britannica* 15th Ed. v8, 221

George Hale Cotton

Paid Dr. Lansing $10.00 on class account for Missions. Attended preaching in the chapel. Mr. Cotton[21] — on text "God is a Spirit" — very good sermon & well delivered.

Wrote for the press in evening.

Recd. letter from S. Joldersma & from A.B.R.

Retired after reading Greek Testament.

𝒮

April, Thursday 26. 1888.

Attended Recitations & taught Alec. Hardenberg.

𝒮

April, Friday 27. 1888.

Attended Recitations.

The class except Mr. Andrew & myself were not prepared & hence Dr. Mabon left in great rage!

Quite an excitement.

First trouble at the Seminary with our class.

---

[21]   George Hale Cotton (1857-1939), New Brunswick Theological Seminary, 1891. HD, 79

Attended a Social in the evening at Mrs. Angeline Pleasant, & dull time!

Got home very late.

♫

April, Saturday 28. 1888.

Wrote at my Dutch Sermon this A.M. Returned books to the library.

Called on Dr. Mabon this A.M. He asked me to visit Dr. Drury in reference to Agency for the Xtian Intelligencer.

Spend P.M. in a walk & a call on Mrs. Doolitte — pleasant talker. Received an invitation to call on her with Brother F.J.Z. Went to Dr. Drury in evening & made arrangements to visit the churches West of Rochester for the Xtian Intelligencer. Am to receive $1.00 a subscriber & a bonus in case I obtain more than $200 as subscribtion money. Or rather 200 subscribers. Retired after reading Bible at 10.30.

♫

April, Sunday 29. 1888.

Attended Services in Suydam St. Church. Dr. Ten Eyck[22] "I know that my Redeemer liveth." Good but poor delivery because read.

Diner at C. Hardenbergh. S.S. 7 in my class – Spoke on Missions to them. Afternoon service Dr. Ten Eyck "Almost thou persuadest me to be a Xtian" Innauguration & installa' of elders & deacons.

Prayer-Meeting; Mr. Sharpley leader.

Went to Lecture (Vth of the Vedder course) Dr. Cooper : Doubt Suicidal (see lectures) Reported them for Daily Fredonian.

Retired at 10.30 P.M.

♫

April, Monday 30. 1888.

Attended Recitations in A.M. Wrote report for lecture & took it to Fredonian Office. Tutored Alex Hardenbergh in his various branches of study.

---

[22] William Hoffman Ten Eyck (1818-1908), Permanent Clerk, General Synod, 1871-1907. HD, 390

May 1888

May, Tuesday 1. 1888.

Recitations.
Read essay for Dr. Mabon on the Church Standards.
Read Greek with Rev. Willis
Taught my pupil.
Read & studied in P.M.

Wrote at Dutch Sermon in evening & attended Arabic recitations at Dr. Lansing's.

$\mathcal{g}$

May, Wednesday 2. 1888.

Attended Recitation's
Meeting of Soc. of Inquiry in evening. On my motion the meeting adjourned to Mrs. Bradley's and we had cream & cake.
Very pleasant evening.

$\mathcal{g}$

May, Thursday 3. 1888.

Attended Recitations.
Wrote Letters. Studied & wrote essay for Dr. Mabon.

Tutoring $10.00

$\mathcal{g}$

May, Friday 4. 1888.

Attended last Recitations of the year. Examinations to begin next Tuesday.

Tutored my pupil & received $10.00 payment on account. Received an invitation from Dr. West[1] to preach for the church at the Palisades N.J. Accepted. Wrote letter to A.B. Reid. Made a call on Dr. Mabon & spoke with him on the Western Seminary & its needs.
Retired late.

---

[1] Jacob West (1818-1890), Corresponding Secretary, Board of Domestic Missions, 1868-1888. HD, 460

$\mathcal{Z}$

May, Saturday 5. 1888.

Arose at 6.00

Took train at 7.20 for New York. Visited General Conference of M.E. Church in the Metropolitan Opera House. Grand Body of men. Bought photograph of Bishop Taylor[2].

Called at Synod Rooms & Intelligencer Office. Took dinner at the Palace Hotel on invitation of George Mabon. Pleasant time.

Took a stroll along the docks. inspected the Brittania anchor line; fine steamer. Went to Wharf foot of Canal St & took Str. Fort Lee for Palisades. Met Elder Van Slyke & was received at the home of Person's. Miss Edina P.[3] is mistress of the home.

Spent evening in Singing & Conversation.

$\mathcal{Z}$

May, Sunday 6. 1888.

Arose at 6.00 Spent a season in prayer. Read over Sermons. Breakfast with the Persons. Pleasant people. Church service at the chapel at 11 A.M. Small but attentive audience. Was greatly helped in prayer & speech. Text. John 8:12. Dinner. Stroll with Miss. P. in the woods – beautiful Scenery. S.S. in P.M. Mr. Willam a pleasant xtian Quaker is Supb. Spoke to the children on Home Missions. Took a walk along the Palisades with Elder Van Slyke. Fine view of the Hudson. Supper. Preached in evening <u>without</u> <u>notes</u> on John 4:10.

Pleasant service. God's mercies are faithful & true to those that trust in him. Glass of milk & cracker — Welcome Rest.

$\mathcal{Z}$

May, Monday 7. 1888.

Arose at 5 A.M. Read lectures in Review for Examination. Breakfast. Str. for Fort Lee at 7.30. Purchased some books at a cheap store on Canal Street _ Book of Prayer & Vulgate Testament.

Bought pair of shoes $3.00 at **Serwys** – Broadway.

2   Bishop William Taylor (1821-1902), Missionary to Africa.www.scribd.com/doc/120693454/Legacy-of-William-Taylor?secret_password=277ew475vat0c0pi9b6m

3   Edina Person (1869-?), Student at Cooper Union. *The Twenty-Ninth Annual Report of the Trustees of the Cooper Union for the Advancement of Science and Art*. New York: Brokaw & Atwater, Stationers and Printers, 54 Broad Street 1888, 62.

David D. Demarest

Took Ferry & Train at 11:15 A.M. Dinner at New Brunswick. Taught Alec Hardenbergh. Reviewed Lessons for Examination.

Very busy with preparing two sermons for next Sabbath as well as preparation for Examinations. Retired late.

May, Tuesday 8. 1888.

Arose at 6 A.M. Studied. Made outline of sermon on Ascension of Christ.

Pleasant time when taking a walk with Mr. F.R. Scudder. Got some wild-flowers for the dinner table.

Received program of Order of Examinations.

Dr. Demarest from 2 ½ – 4 this afternoon – quite difficult but I could answer all the 14 questions.

Called on Dr. Lansing & paid him $10. more on Missionary Subscription. Met Dr. Waters etc.

Spent evening in writing and complete sketch of sermon on Acts 1:9-11 for next Sabbath.

The Heidelbergh Catechism is fine on the Ascension of Xt.

May, Wednesday 9. 1888.

Examinations in
Dr. Mabon &

Dr. Woodbridge

5 hours of hard work.

Taught Alec Hardenbergh.

May, Thursday 10. 1888.

Examinations to-day 5 ½ hours with Profs. DeWitt & Lansing.

Taught Alec Hardenbergh.

Attended lecture-course of Aggazzi Association[4].

Mr. Ferini[5] (Lulu) gave an illustrated lecture on Central Africa & his journeys thither. He went as a show-man to find diamonds — Moffat went as a missionary to find pearls – What a difference in errand!
People will always cry hurrah at a show-man & extol his wonderful bravery while Moffat is scarcely <u>hea</u>rd of:

Wrote at <u>Sermons</u>.

May, Friday 11. 1888.

Examinations all over. Studied at Sermons & attended to tutoring of Alec Hardenberg in A.M.

Had a Seminary debate in P.M. in Hertzog Hall Chapel on Subject: "Res. that the need of workers is greater in the Foreign than in the home field." Opened the debate in the affirmative. Excitement ran high. Took train at 5.10 for New York. Ferry for Hoboken. Car to Union Hill. Supper at the home of Rev. Gowen. Pleasant evening in Conversation

---

[4]   Likely the Agassiz Association. *Science An Illustrated Journal*, Volume XII, New York, N.D.C. Hodges, 1888.
[5]   Samuel Wasgate (1855-?) adopted son of showman William Leonard Hunt (the Great Farini) he often performed under the guise Lulu Farini, a woman.www.metafilter.com/104905/Lulu-Farini-cannonball-in-drag

with Misses G. & Rev. Spoke with him on Missions & their Need. Retired at 11 P.M.

Pleasant Stay.

☞

May, Saturday 12. 1888.

Spent A.M. in reading etc. Heard of the Sudden death of Clarence Scudder[6] in the Hertzog Hall Gymnasium. Went in company with Mr. & Mrs. Gowen to New York. Dinner at Evert's Restaur. Call at Cook's & at a cheap book store. Boat Ft. Lee for Coytesville. (Linwood).
Was entertained at the home of Person's.
Spent evening in music & in warbling a warble.

☞

May, Sunday 13. 1888.

Attended Service in A.M. Preached from Acts 1:9-12.
Ascension-Day.
Rainy morning & small audience.
Attended S.School. Taught Bible Class for Miss Person. Spoke to the children. Dinner. Met Miss. Sarth...[?]. A pleasant & witty lady — friend of Person's.
Preached in Evening on I Cor. 15:58. — xtian activity.
Larger audience than A.M.

☞

May, Monday 14. 1888.

Stage for Ft. Lee.
Boat for New York.
Visit at Synod Rooms etc. taught Alec Hardenbergh. Read & Wrote letters.

☞

[6] Clarence Scudder (1869-1888), son of Jared Waterbury Scudder, died in College. Corwin, 721

Araki Miyake

~~Fun. 3 P.M.~~
May, Tuesday 15. 1888.

Attended Funeral of Clarence Scudder who died from a gymnasium accident.

Fine service & very impressive.

Examinations to-day — Oral , before <u>the Bd. Of Sup'tendents</u>.
Spent the Evening in writing sermons etc.

May, Wednesday 16. 1888.

Examinations in A.M. Alumnus dinner at 2 P.M. 79 present — pleasant time & good after-dinner speeches — especially by Dr. Doolittle & Dr. Drury. Commencement Exercises in Evening — Acted as usher in 1st Ref. Ch. Small audience.

Mr. Miyaki[7] had a good speech on Foreign Missions. Retired early.

---

7   Araki Miyake (1865-1902), New Brunswick Theological Seminary, 1888. Raven, 158

May, Thursday 17. 1888.

Spent day in reading & study.

Called on Dr. Woodbridge in evening.

♋

May, Friday 18. 1888.

Worked at Sermons & article for "De Hope" in A.M. Taught Pupil in P.M.

Attended Y.P. Union of 4th Ref. Church in evening & was elected President for the ensuing year. Took bath & retired at 11 P.M.

♋

May, Saturday 19. 1888.

Arose at 6 A.M. Wrote for Press. Answered letters etc. Took train at 10:45 for New York.

Visited Synod Rooms & Xtian Intelligencer Office. Took Elevated R.R. for Union Theol. Seminary.

Visited Central Park, Menagerie etc. Took 5th Ave coach for Canal St. Boat for Ft. Lee. Evening in reading & music.

♋

(Written by Miss E Person for me)
May, Sunday 20. 1888.

Arose at - ?

Preached to the Coytesvillan — a very good sermon probably. (can't vouch for that didn't hear it. E.P.) <u>Dinner.</u> Sunday School next – made the girls do something the boys were afraid to do. Delightful time with Mr. Williams[8] before & after. A very frivalous walk home in the woods. Another sermon (Ditto) ~~Homesick~~.

♋

---

8   Marshall Williams (1873-1940), Rutgers College, 1894. Rutgers, 219

May, Monday 21. 1888.

Train for New York.

Received appointment to speak on Foreign Missions at every opportunity & to receive travelling expenses as remuneration.

Called at Intelligencer Office.

Purchased a Cruden at Leggatt Brothers. 81 Chambers.

Train for home.
Read & Studied.

Commenced to read novel by Victor Hugo – Les Miserable. Very Interesting.

*

May, Tuesday 22. 1888.

Studied. Wrote sermon sketches. Made a beginning on "Prayer" Phil. 4:6.

Have a severe head-ache. Attended Prayer-Meeting in evening & heard a fine exposition of Ps. 19 by Dr. Campbell.

Retired after a long talk with Isaac Sperling on Foreign Missions. He expects to enter the For. Field. How many-sided the question is: Where shall I invest my life? May God help me to decide it aright. Rather may my decision already made receive his approval & blessing.

*

May, Wednesday 23. 1888.

Studied Read & prepared sermons for next Sabbath.

*

May, Thursday 24. 1888.

[No Entry]

*

May, Friday 25. 1888.

Read Les Miserables & worked at translation for Board of Foreign Missions "How Hindu Christians give.

Very pleasant time in evening in reading & writing letters.

♪

May, Saturday 26. 1888.

Took train at 9.19 for New York. Visited Fulton Street Prayer Meeting for an hour. Pleasant Meeting Room cosy. good singing Mottoes on wall: Jesus only. In God we trust: Bethel Peniel: Many took part; so did I.

Dinner at Restaurant. Synods Rooms; Met Rev. Stone etc.

Took walk with F.S. Scudder Steamer for Ft. Lee at 5 P.M. Supper at Mrs. Person's. Miss Edina P. sketched a sod-house for me in charcoal from a photograph. Will use it to illustrate "Home – Missions."

Retired after some music on the piano at 11 P.M.

♪

May, Sunday 27. 1888.

Arose at 7.30. Breakfast. Looked over Sermon sketch Phillipians 4:6: Prayer. Quite good attendance in A.M. Visited Mr. Willam after Sabbath School in P.M. Pleasant chat.

Took walk in the woods with Miss. E.P. & got some wild flowers.

After tea went to church & hung up pictures & maps to illustrate the Frontier work.

Spoke on Josh 13:1 in connection with the work in the West. Large gathering. Mr. Willam blessed me a la Jacob when the meeting closed; then doxology. Last of Ft. Lee for some time. Have enjoyed it very much. Promised to call again. Retired after music & conversation.

♪

May, Monday 28. 1888.

Steamer at 7.30 for Canal St. New York in company with Miss. P. visited Cooper Union[9] where she is studying art.

[9] Cooper Union endowed by Peter Cooper in 1859 as an undergraduate college. *Britannica* 15th Ed. v3, 605

Visited Book – stores etc. & purchased volume to present to P.J.Z. at Commencement. Purchased satchel for $4.50 at Courtland St. W. of Broadway.

Dinner with Mr. Scudder at Armstrongs. 178 B'dway. Train at 3 P.M. homeward. Studied & read mail. Called on Dr. Lansing & Dr. Demarest in evening. Pleasant hour. Received from Dr. D. a copy of Centennial Volume of Theol. Sem. at New Brunswick. Retired at 11 P.M.

Heavy thunder – shower.

May, Tuesday 29. 1888.

Worked & Read up for Missions. Wrote sketch of thoughts on Missions in Dutch.

Spent evening in my room.

Gave last lesson to Alec Hardenbergh & promised to come again next year if nothing hinders.

May, Wednesday 30. 1888.

Decoration Day! Read Les Miserables by Victor Hugo.

Mrs. J.J. Van Zanten[10] called at my room at 12 o'clock & with him I visited the city & called on Dr. Mabon etc.

Took tea with the Dr. & remained over night. Pleasant stay.

May, Thursday 31. 1888.

Took train at 9:29 for New York City. Visited & secured a room in company with Mr. V.Z. At 131 E. 31st Street. Made a visit of many public buildings etc.

[10]   Jacob J. Van Zanten (1858-1908), WTS, 1890. HD, 438

June 1888

June, Friday 1. 1888.

Spent day in sightseeing in and around New York. Visited statue of liberty on Bedloe's Island.

Very imposing sight. Brother Fred came in town from Dakota to-day. Attended evening lecture in Collegiate Church in Evening.

♋

June, Saturday 2. 1888.

Spent day in New York

Went to Port Richmond Staten Island and took dinner at Mrs. E.B. Horton's. Pleasant time. Spoke with Mrs. E.B. on Home Missions. Left at 10.30 & arrived at New York at 12.00.

♋

June, Sunday 3. 1888.

Attended church services to-day. A.M. Dr. H. Crosby[1] & Parkhurst. P.M. heard Secty. Warburton on Social Purity. & visited R.R. Y.M.C.A.

Attended service at Brooklyn Tabernacle in evening. Text: "Sufficent to the day is the evil thereof".

Talmadge was not at his best.

♋

June, Monday 4. 1888.

Left New York at 10 A.M. for New Brunswick. Packed trunk & made some farewell calls. Had a pleasant time on the train with Bros. F.J.Z. Went to Weehawken P. C. & spent night at Rev. I.W. Gowen Very social time.

Fire in evening at Guttenberg near bye.

♋

June, Tuesday 5. 1888.

Left Grove Parsonage at 10 A.M. train for New York. Called at Synod Rooms Received $10 from Rev. H.N. Cobb D sl. on account. Called at Mrs. Sandham on 45th street

---

[1] Howard Crosby(1826-1891), Presbyterian Clergyman and Professor of Rutgers. Rutgers, 40

Took Elevated R.R. For port of Jay St. where we took "Kaaterskill" Steamer for Catskill. Arrived there at 5 A.M.

$$\mathcal{Z}$$

June, Wednesday 6. 1888.

Am staying at the Prospect Park Hotel. Many delegates to Genl. Synod have already arrived.

The hotel is first-class in all respects.

Attended meeting of Synod in A.M. Rev. M.H. Hutton was elected President. & P. Moerdyke[2] vice president.

No business was transacted.

Rev. Shepherd[3] preached the sermon in the evening from Acts 1:3. Quite good but very long & tedious.

Heavy thunder-shower in evening.

$$\mathcal{Z}$$

June, Thursday 7. 1888.

Attended sessions of Synod. Heard discussion on Liturgy—question quite animated. Synod sent greetings to Holland with Rev. Dosker[4]. & also cablegram to London Miss'y Conference. Wrote at Translation in evening. Very pleasant time.

Met Mr. & Mrs. Van Cleef. She is a nice social lady & enjoys hearing about the "West" etc. Brother F.J.Z. _ "the Missionary from Dakota is quite lionized here. Retired in Room 19 at 12 M.

$$\mathcal{Z}$$

June, Friday 8. 1888.

Attended sessions of Synod. Evening meeting was on Sabbath Schools & on Catechisms & instruction. Revs. Williamson[5] & Peter Moerdyke made stirring speeches especially the latter. He emphasized the importance of Catechetical Instruction above the S.S. & its machinery.

---

2 Peter Moerdyke (1845-1923), Pastor, First, Grand Rapids, MI, 1873-1892. HD, 271
3 Charles Isaac Shepherd (1827-1903), Pastor, Newtown, NY, 1867-91. HD, 358
4 Henry Elias Dosker (1855-1926), Lecturer, WTS, 1884-1888. HD, 110
5 William Hall Williamson (1855-1905), Pastor, Tappan, NY. 1883-1889. HD, 467

Was asked by Dr. H.E. Cobb to speak next Monday night before Synod on the Student Volunteer question. Declined with thanks. Would like to have had the opportunity but I fear I shall hurt myself by making people think I seek prominence.

Retired with Bros. F.J.Z. At 11.30 P.M.

♗

June, Saturday 9. 1888.

Attended Session of Synod. No special business.

Paid Bill at Hotel & went after dinner with Rev. E.A. Collier[6] & Rev. Cox to Kinderhook N.Y. to speak on children's day. Spoke with Mr. Boyd Supt. Am. Bible Soc & found work for P.J.Z. for summer. Ferry to Hudson Station Train to Stuyvesant & thence by stage-line to Kinderhook. Pleasant little village; population largely retired merchants etc. Two banks & printing establishment. Spent evening in conversation & music.

Took walk, to Cemetery & saw Van Buren Monument. President Van Buren's residence is near Kinderhook.

Retired at 11:30.

♗

June, Sunday 10. 1888.

Arose at 7 A.M. Attended service in Kinderhook Church. Rev. H.M. Cox[7]. addressed the children in the A.M. Church is very old (1727.) Address good. Rehearsed after service for evening (!)

Spent P.M. in reading etc.

Addressed S.S. in evening Subject "Let your light shine" [candle talk illustration]

Children seemed to enjoy it very much.

Examined old church records of Kinderhook & received an old sermon for a present dated 1797 in the holland language — (manuscript.)

♗

---

[6] Edward Augustus Collier (1835-1920), Pastor, Kinderhook, NY, 1864-1907. HD, 73
[7] Henry Miller Cox (1854-1916), Pastor, Herimer, NY, 1882-90, Superintendent, New Brunswick Theological Seminary, 1888-90. HD, 80

June, Monday 11. 1888.

Arose at 7.00. Received $5 from Rev. Collier for my work. Took stage-line to Stuyvezant & then train for Catskill station. Met Miss. Anderson — a real pleasant old maid. Attended Synod in P.M. no special business.

Evening session of Synod was in behalf of Foreign Missions. Good. Rev. Ballagh[8], Rev. Scudder, L.R. Scudder, & Rev. Sawyer spoke on the subject.

Rev. Cobb had asked me to speak, but I declined.

June, Tuesday 12. 1888.

Attended sessions of Synod. Synod voted $110000.00 at least for Foreign Missions! Good, but not enough for the ability of our church. At the afternoon session a ballot was taken for a Professor at Holland Theol. Seminary. Rev. J.W. Beardslee D.D[9]. received at second ballot 102 votes & was therefore declared elected. How strange things form out. Who would have dreamed 8 years ago that theology would be restored at Hope & that Rev. Steffens[10] & Beardslee would be its instructors!!!

This evening addresses were made on behalf of Domestic Missions by Rev. Gamble[11], F.J. Zwemer and Beardslee

Brother F.J. did himself credit. and was applauded heartily.

June, Wednesday 13. 1888.

Attended Synod-sessions. No important business. After dinner I packed my satchel & took omnibus for Steamboat Station.

The scenery along the Hudson & about Prospect Park is grand. I am sorry however that I could not take a trip up the mountains.

Arrived at Albany at 6 P.M. Took State Street car to Hamilton St. Tea at Mrs. Dykstra

Met many old friends. Albany of 12 years ago is nearly the same!

---

[8]   James Hamilton Ballagh (1832-1920), Missionary, Japan, 1861-1920. HD, 16

[9]   John Walter Beardslee (1837-1921), Pastor, North, West Troy, NY, 1884-88, Professor, WTS, 1888-1917. HD, 20

[10] Nicholas M. Steffens (1839-1912), Professor, WTS, 1884-1895. HD, 374

[11] Samuel Landis Gamble (1828-1895), Stated Supply, First Pekin, IL, 1885-1890. HD, 142

Spoke on For. Missions in Holland language before a moderate audience in evening. Found some, but not much trouble with finding words to express myself. Retired at 12 M.

♫

June, Thursday 14. 1888.

Spent A.M. In a visit to the Albany Capitol.

Very beautiful building — especially the Assembly Room — but also a sample of American Architecture — not durable.

Spoke before the women of the church at Jay St. & recommended the support of a native teacher. Distributed Missy. literature & took some subscriptions for Mission Field.

Supper at Mrs. De Rouville. (Le Daai)

Called on Mr. Phelps in evening & was very kindly received. Annie is an invalid. Retired after writing letters etc.

♫

June, Friday 15. 1888.

Took train at 8:25 for Rochester. Mr. Van Drielle for company. Made a pleasant acquaintance on the road Miss. Porter of Farmersville, N.Y.

Took stop-over at Syracuse. Visited Y.M.C.A. & saw town.

Train at 4:55 for Rochester. Found quarters at the Temperance Hotel 212 E. Main St.

Very good, clear. Xtian place. to stay.

Retired after writing some letters.

♫

June, Saturday 16. 1888.

Arose early; took bath & shave. Breakfast. Surface-car for 49 Concord Ave Rev. P. De. Bruins[12]. Saw City in company with Revs. Van Doren[13] & Broek[14] in P.M. Powers art Gallery.

---

[12]   Peter De Bruyn, (1850-1897), Pastor Rochester, NY, 1873-1891. HD, 89
[13]   David Kline Van Doren (1841-1908), Pastor, Middleburgh, NY. 1885-1890 HD, 418
[14]   John Broek (1841-1922), Pastor, Milwaukee, WI, 1884-1893. HD, 49

Simon Marinus Hogenboom

Took train at 3.07 P.M. for Palmyra. Stage for Marion. Received very kindly by S. Hoogeboom[15]. Mrs. H is very pleasant.

Spent evening in conversation & in rehearsing "Auld Lang Syne" & College days.

Rev. H. asked me to conduct both services tomorrow. Accepted.

※

June, Sunday 17. 1888.

Breakfast. S.S. service at 10.30. Church at 12 M.

Spoke in Holland Language on Acts 16:9.

Large attendance — full house. Was greatly helped in speaking.

Succeeded in interesting both Shepherd & Flock. Last year this church gave average .05 per per member to For. Missions!!

Hope to see a change next year. Rested in P.M. & read Van Oostezee's[16] Practical Theology.

Meeting in evening. Missy lecture — maps, photographs etc. Interested audience & speaker. I am beginning to feel more free in public.

[15]   Simon Marinus Hogenboom (1858-1935), Pastor, Marion, NY, 1887-1890. (Multiple Spellings of last name exist. Hogeboom, Hoogeboom, Hogenboom, Hoogenboom) HD, 182

[16]   Jan Jacob van Oosterzee (1817-1882), Professor of Theology, University of Utrecht. *Encyclopædia Britannica*, 1911, Volume 20, 120

Met consistory after service & after a cup of tea at the parsonage retired.

⚬

June, Monday 18. 1888.

Rev. S. Hoogeboom drove me to depot at 7 A.M. Wrote letters while waiting for train. Train at 9.30 for Rochester. Arrived at R. at 10.45. Went to Rev. P. De Bruin who took me to Mr. A.W. Hopeman[17] where I am now staying. He is a contractor, quite wealthy & very pleasant & social. The family had a severe loss in the death of their son John last fall.

Took a drive with their coach-man in the evening. Pleasant drive & good company. Retired late.

⚬

June, Tuesday 19. 1888.

Spent A.M. In driving through Rochester in company with Mr. Hopeman.

Saw new 2nd Ref. Church etc.

Visited Power's Art Gallery in P.M. Very fine in its collection & arrangement. "The Temptation of "St. Anthony." & the "Vespers in Kindergarten" were especially fine.

Spent evening in calling on Friends & secured a few subscribers to the Xtian Intelligencer. Van de Korde's are very kind people & remember Father & Mother when they were at Rochester.

⚬

June, Wednesday 20. 1888.

Spent A.M. in a drive along East Avenue.

Dinner at Rev. Van der Hart's[18]. He seemed to find fault with my studying Theol. In the East instead of at Holland Mich.

Secured one subscriber to the Xtian Intelligencer. After tea at Hopeman's called for Rev. P. De B.[19] & went with him to Union Meeting

---

[17] Arendt Willem Hopeman (1843-1928), Owner A.W. Hopeman & Sons Company, Builders, Rochester, New York. www.myheritage.com/research/record-40001-101 9600891/arendt-willem-hopeman-in-familysearch-family-tree?s=542832841
[18] Evert Vander Hard (1847-1889), Pastor, Second, Rochester, NY, 1887-89. HD, 409
[19] Likely Peter De Bruyn (1850-1897), Pastor, Rochester, NY, 1873-91. HD, 89

at 1ˢᵗ Ref. Chapel in behalf of For. Missions. Spoke 20 min. in Dutch &
15 in English on <u>The</u> Subject of the hour. Was not as fluent as I wished
& did not seem as confident as I was at Marion or Albany.

I did not pray enough — that so<u>lves the</u> difficulty.

Distributed Missy. Literature.

ᘒ

June, Thursday 21. 1888.

Took train at 8.15 for Buffalo. Purchased 1ˢᵗ Class Ticket on Mich.
Central & Lake Shore to Grand Rapids from Rochester for $12.25

Stopped at Buffalo for 3 hrs. Saw Soldier's Monument & St. Paul's
Cathederal with its grand organ (Centennial 1876). Train at 2 P.M. for
Brockton Jc. & thence to Clymer.

One of Rev. Van Doren's Sons met me at Clymer St. & we went by
buggy to parsonage. Mrs. V. D. is very pleasant. Thunder-Shower kept
some people from church. Union Meeting with Abbe Church. Large
attendance. Was helped in speaking & found pleasure in seeing my
audience interested.

Met Dr. Reinsberger!
Where will he go next?

ᘒ

June, Friday 22. 1888.

Visited Rev. Hoffman[20] & family. Clymer has 3 churches & only
400 population. Brockton has 650 population & only 5 churches! All
Evangelical with one exception.

Went from Clymer to Brockton & am now at the Best hotel at the
place — a bar-room concern. Waiting for trains is disagreeable work.

ᘒ

June, Saturday 23. 1888.

From Brockton to Cleveland. Remained at home of Mr. Nahuis—
very pleasant family.

Saw city in P.M. & evening.
Garfield Monument etc.

---

[20] John Hoffman (1849-1930), Pastor, Abbe, Clymer, NY, 1887-1893. HD, 181

❧

June, Sunday 24. 1888.

Preached in A.M. At East Side church & in P.M. on West Side Good audiences on both occasions. Spoke in Dutch both times.

Heard a young Presb. student in evening. poor thought & delivery.

❧

June, Monday 25. 1888.

From Cleveland at 5.45 A.M. To Holland via Allegan where arrived at 6 P.M. Attended lilfilas Club meeting etc. Very good.

Met P.J.Z. & the sisters.

❧

June, Thursday 26. 1888.

Spent day in Holland & visited Mary at the Park. Ben & she are still enjoying life.

Attended Alumni exercises in evening & found them very enjoyable. The Chronicles were especially good.

❧

June, Wednesday 27. 1888.

Spent A.M. in calling on Friends. P.M. ditto Commencement exercises in Evening were good
Peter's Valedictory capped the climax.
Was appointed this A.M. by Alumni association to prepare a college song. Accepted.
Rainy & disagreeable day.

❧

June, Thursday 28. 1888.

Spent day in calling on friends etc.

John Walter Beardslee

Called on Dr. Chas. Scott[21] in evening. Met Rev. Beardslee Prof. elect of the Seminary.

♪

June, Friday 29. 1888.

Attended Picnic of Hope Church S.S. Pleasant time & met many acquaintances.

Took train at 6 P.M. for Gd. Rapids. Arrived there in company with Kate & James & their children. Pleasant family Reunion.

♪

June, Saturday 30. 1888.

Called on Rev. P. Moerdyk & was asked to preach for him in the evening.

He wished to see me on the Western Seminary Question!!
He did. No results. Called on Friends in P.M. John Trompen[22] owns a clothing Store on Grandville Ave.

[21]   Charles Scott (1822-1893), President, Hope College, 1885-92. HD, 351
[22]   John N. Trompen (1865-1940), Merchant and Business owner.

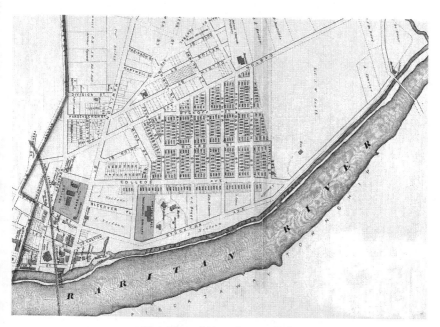

The City of New Brunswick

Hertzog Hall, New Brunswick Theological Seminary

Gardner A. Sage Library,
New Brunswick Theological
Seminary

James Cantine, John Gulian Lansing, Samuel Marinus Zwemer

July 1888

July, Sunday 1. 1888.

Attended Service in 5th Ref. Ch. in A.M. Rev. Joldersma[1]. Very loud in delivery & not too rich in thought. Preached for him in the afternoon. Text Acts 16:9 in Dutch. Was helped greatly in answer to earnest prayer. I had complete control of myself & my stammering tongue.

Preached in 1st Ref. Ch. in evening. Large attendance: I Cor. 15:88 Pleasant people & a pushing agressive spirit in pulpit & pew.

Walked home with Jno. Trompen.

9

July, Monday 2. 1888.

Spent day in canvassing for the xtian Intelligencer.

Called on Rev. Moerdyke & Rev. Winter[2].
Was asked to preach for him next Sunday evening.

Spent evening at Mr. & Mrs. Ten Hope where I took supper. Pleasant time & social pleasure. Retired late; came home on Cable-Car. System not as good as at <u>Chicago</u>.

9

July, Tuesday 3. 1888.

Spent day in Canvassing but secured only a few orders. Went to drive at Rev. Moerdyke's & Met Mrs. & Miss. M. Pleasant hour.

Took train for Reeds Lake in P.M.
Called at 139 Cass St. in evening & found that the Reeds had just come home.

Pleasant time in talking of Auld Lang Syne etc. Miss. A.B.R. Was as attractive as ever. Asked her to take a ride with me on Thursday evening. Accepted. Went back to S. Joldersma & sister Chris where I am stopping. They have a pleasant home.

9

[1] Rense Henry Joldersma (1854-1913), Pastor, Fifth, Grand Rapids, MI, 1886-89. HD, 200
[2] Egbert Winter (1836-1906), Pastor, Second, Grand Rapids, MI, 1884-95. HD, 469

Egbert Winter

July, Wednesday 4. 1888.

Independence Day! once more. A day of rest for agents & students.

Spent A.M. in letter-writing & went down-town to see the procession. Gd. Rapids celebrated its 50 years birthday. Quite a stir in the city.

Sye & Chris are gone & I have the house to myself. Have resolved to spend the day writing for Missions.

Wrote article for Mission Field & answered correspondents.

ℭ

July, Thursday 5. 1888.

Canvassed for xtian Intelligencer in A.M. & spent P.M. in calling etc. Took tea with Mr. & Mrs. Ten Hope.

Evening in Reading.

Spoke with Fire Dept. on my new patent for communication between nozzle man & engine. Approved.

ℭ

July, Friday 6. 1888.

Spent day in canvassing but had only small success.

ℐ

July, Saturday 7. 1888.

Spent A.M. in rest & reading.
Attended Picnic at Reeds lake with the Reeds in afternoon.

Pleasant hour. Miss. A.B.R. & I had an open-hearted talk which explained matters & did us both good.

A tempores a mores.

Spent evening in reading & writing. Retired at 11.30 P.M.

ℐ

July, Sunday 8. 1888.

Attended church in A.M. Rev. Tupper. Baptist. Very good sermon — rational on Jethro's words to Moses. Attended Baptism ceremony. Not very impressive. Too much inconvenience for prayer etc. Is manner of Baptism a non-essential?

Took dinner at Rev. De Prees[3] Happy family _ 12 children! Spoke in P.M. before a large congregation on Hana 16:9. (Dutch)

Took tea at Rev. De Pree's. Walked to Bostwick St. to Rev. Winter's church. Preached evening sermon (English) on John 8:12. Was greatly helped in my delivery. Walked home with Sye & Chris.

Watermelon treat.

Retired at 10.30.

Pleasant Sabbath Day!

ℐ

July, Monday 9. 1888.

Arose at 6 A.M. Took train at 9 A.M. for Holland. Boat for Park — Shady Side Landing. Dinner at Brother Beri's. Pleasant re-union of Brothers & sisters. Made a visit to Mr. Lugers in P.M. Spent evening in conversation & talk on Missions. Retired early & fell tired. This vacation is certainly not a vacancy for me.

ℐ

---

[3] Peter De Pree (1839-1915), Pastor, Fourth Grand Rapids, MI, 1882-1891. HD, 99

July, Tuesday 10. 1888.

Went to Holland with 9.30 Boat.
Called at Hope Office & at Mrs. Panels.

Went calling with sisters Nellie & Rika in P.M. Le Febre's, Doesburg, Kollen, Scott etc.
Spent evening in writing for the press.

§

July, Wednesday 11. 1888.

Spent day in Holland. canvassing for the Xtian Intelligencer.

Supper at Ye Rollers. Spent evening in calling.
Very busy still.

§

July, Thursday 12. 1888.

Spent A.M. at Holland. Called on Allcott's etc.

Walked to Graafschap & had bread & milk dinner at Strabbing's[4].

Took drive with Henrietta & Nellie around Graafschap. Called on Neerken's & Rev. John.[5] Mrs. John gave me some German Missy tracts. Pleasant hour at Strabbings.

§

July, Friday 13. 1888.

Walked to Holland & canvassed xtian Intelligencer.
Visited Rev. Steffens S.D. Alberta etc. & wrote letters.
Gave Bloemendaal[6] instructions relative to my trunk.
Took boat at 6 P.M. for Park – Shady Side.
Pleasant time with Brother Ben & the Sisters.
Retired early & feel very tired. My motto has become a reality:

"Repos Ailleurs[7]"

4   Albert H. Strabbing (1856-1954), WTS, 1889. HD, 379
5   C.C.A.L. John (1840-1915), Pastor, Graafschap, MI, 1887-1891. HD, 198
6   Ralph Bloemendaal (1859-1929), WTS, 1889. HD, 34
7   Repos Ailleurs: (French) Rest Elsewhere

Carl Christopher Alexandre Logren
(C.C.A.L.) John

July, Saturday 14. 1888.

Boat at 9 A.M. for Depot. Met Prof. Kollen. & had a pleasant chat with him. Train for Allegan. Walked to village. Met Mr. Thew[8] & was very agreeably entertained by Mrs. Thew[9]. Charlie[10] was not at home.

Dinner at Thews.

Train at 4.12 P.M. for Kalamazoo.

Rev. Vennema[11] met me at the train & took me to stay at one of his parishoners _ Mr. Van Hoolden.

Pleasant young people. 2 children Annie & Leonard.

Leonard is a bright — mischievous fellow & full of fun.

Called at Y.M.C.A. Rooms.

July, Sunday 15. 1888.

Arose at 7 A.M. Breakfast. Attended Installation service at 1st Ref.

[8]   Joseph J. Thew (1830-1898), was a Circuit Court Commisioner in New York, 1880.
[9]   Sophia Adeline Thew (1841-1927), Housekeeper, wife of Joseph and mother of Charles, Bessie, and Jessie.
[10] Charles N. Thew (1865-1927)
[11] Ame Vennema (1857-1925), Pastor, Second, Kalamazoo, MI, 1886-89. HD, 441

Ch. — Rev. Kolÿn[12]. Rev. De Pree's sermon was very good & logical. He has wonderful control of the Holland Language.

Dinner. Spoke before the Y.M.C.A. on Missions.

In Evening I spoke at Rev. Vennema's church. on Foreign Missions. 320 in audience.

Was helped in speaking in answer to prayer. Spent pleasant hour at Mr. Van Hoolen 323 Davis St. Kalamazoo.

§

July, Monday 16. 1888.

Called on Rev. Kolÿn & helped lay carpets. Pleasant time at supper.

Received list of Subscribers & names to expect to commence work to-morrow.

Find little time in vacation to write in my diary. My time for leisure is so short that I am falling into the terrible habit of cutting short my devotional duties.

Bible Reading when one skips from place to place is hard work.

§

July, Tuesday 17. 1888.

Spent day in canvassing for the Xtian Intelligencer. Secured two subscriptions. Spent evening at Mrs. Baels, in company with Anthony Van Drinen Pleasant hour.

§

July, Wednesday 18. 1888.

Spent day in Canvas. Dinner at Kolÿn.

4 subscribers.

Went in evening in company with four young fellows to visit the Stockbridge Estate on invitation.

Elegant house & surroundings. Kalamazoo is a fine place & worthy of all its celebrated renown as a city.

Retired at 10. P.M.

§

[12]   Matthew Kolÿn (1856-1918), Pastor, First, Kalamazoo, MI, 1888-93. HD, 216

July, Thursday 19. 1888.

Arose early. Farewell breakfast at Van Hovleu's with Baldie, Annie Pa & Ma. Pleasant hour.

Secured a new subscriber. Called on Mrs. Latta a lady with whom I staid during the Y.M.C.A. Convention in 1886. Cordial reception. Bouquet. Train for Montana at 9.10 A.M. Rev. Peeke met me & we drove to Centreville with Maud S. I.

Afternoon in social pleasure. Spoke at church in evening on For. Missions. Persuaded them to purchase a Missy. Chart. About 70 were present. & I enjoyed it very much. Retired after music at Peeke Home. Pleasant people to stay with.

July, Friday 20. 1888.

Was invited to accompany Mr. & Mrs. Peeke & Mrs. McKinley (a lively French widow-lady) to a picnic at Fish Lake. Drive of six miles. Pleasant party all day. Boat-riding, sketching, music, etc. Wore Rev. Peekes shoes as mine were at the maker's! Two sizes too large but pleasantry made up for it.

Miss. Baterman sketched the shoes from a fore-view! Drive back with the Batermans. Spent evening in reading & writing. Leave tomorrow for South Bend but have had a most pleasant stay at Centreville.

Miss. Peeke is a little "too beyond" to suit my ideal, "The Girl of the Period".

July, Saturday 21. 1888.

Spent A.M. in calling & letterwriting. Train at 12.40 for Niles. Waited there one hour & ½ to make connections.

Small but busy town. From Niles to South Bend. Pleasant Reception, Rev. Williamson at Depot. Sickness in his family & therefor taken to Misses. Carpenter.

Nice old maids. 4 cats in the house.

Spent evening in reading & conversation.

Before I came to Carpenters I acted as witness to a marriage as Rev. Willamson.

{Mr. John Tio} South Bend 2nd.
{Miss. Reed.}

℥

July, Sunday 22. 1888.

Arose at 7.30. Breakfast. Addressed S.S. in A.M. at nine on For. Missions.

Missy. sermon in A.M. Rev. 3:8.

Good S.S. but poor attendance at church.

Afternoon attended funeral services at house — Rev. Williamson.

Spoke to S.S. in P.M. & after tea preached in evening at Mission Chapel. I Cor. 15:58. Quite a member present. Was helped in speaking, but should not have used a manuscript —

I feel more "on fire" when I do not look on paper.

Attended after-meeting in Baptist Church.

℥

July, Monday 23. 1888.

Spent A.M. in letter writing. Visited Port Office & other buildings. Attended Pastor's Meeting & related Mrs. Rhea's dream on "Missy Fire". Took train after dinner for Chicago.

Got off on stop-over at Valparaiso Ind. & walked to Normal School[13] where I met Mrs. Hofna. Pleasant time. Supper etc. Talk in evening. Slept with one of the students in "De Witt Hall".

About 2000 students attend the school.

The Recital at night was interesting.

℥

July, Thursday 24. 1888.

Left Valparaiso on early train. Breakfast at Restaurant with Mrs. Hofna.

Arrived at Chicago 10.30 Went to Mr. Birkhoff 647 West Harrison St.

Dinner. Called at De Beys. Train for Kensington & thence to Roseland.

Pleasant time at Rev. Van Ess[14]. Received Mail Retired early. Tired & headache.

---

13   Northern Indiana Normal School and Business Institute opened 1873, was Valparaiso Male and Female College which closed in 1871.

14   Balster Van Ess (1844-1900), Pastor, First Roseland, Chicago, IL, 1884-1900. HD, 422

ℰ

July, Wednesday 25. 1888.

Arose at 7.00 A.M. Went fishing with Rev. Van Ess. Wrote letters.

Walked to Fernwood & just missed train at 10 A.M. Dinner at Mr. Vanden Burg. Train for Englewood at 12.40

Met Rev. De Jong [De Jonge][15]. Made arrangements to speak for him on Sunday next. Train at 2.40 for Chicago. Called at 148 Madison & bought Missy chart.

Called at Birkhoffs & left satchel.

Went to Mr. Vernon (who requested me to speak on Missions when he met me at South Bend / 833 W. Monroe. Supper. Pleasant family.

Spoke in Prayer Meeting.

ℰ

July, Thursday 26. 1888.

Slept last night at D. Vernon's. Breakfast & social hour of pleasure. Little Olive Vernon is a sweet girl.

Saw sights this A.M. "Jerusalem on the day of Crucifixtion" — Panorama. Grand & Interesting! Dinner at Rev. DeBey's[16]. Supper at Birkhoffs. Pleasant talk with Mrs. & Jennie Donck etc.

Took car down town. Bristol Hotel: Adams St Room No. 40. Pleasant quarters & quite cleanly. Read Bible & Retired - tired!

ℰ

July, Friday 27. 1888.

Arose at 7.00 A.M. Noisy night near the Depot. Breakfast at Restaurant. Bought tooth-brush & pencil at Fair. Visited 48 Mc Cormmick Black Women's Board v [of] For. Miss. 75 present. Interesting meeting. Spoke in behalf of the Volunteers.

Met Mr. Davis & St. Clair at the Farewell Hall noon meeting. Mr. D. supports 12 missionaries in China. Dinner at [undecipherable scribble ?] Restaurant with them. Called on Mr. Jacobs. Train for Englewood. Cordial Reception at Rev. De Jong's.

[15]   Jacob P. De Jonge (1854-1932), Pastor, Englewood, Chicago, IL, 1887-1893. HD, 94
[16]   Bernardus De Bey (1816-1894), Pastor, Holland, Chicago, IL, 1868-1891. HD, 88

July, Saturday 28. 1888.

Spent day in Englewood. Wrote article for "De Hope" & letters.

Went to Chicago & P.M. in company with Rev. De Jong & had a pleasant time.

Visited Gunther's Museum & saw "a piece of the snake which tempted Eve" — taken from a French R.C. Church & attended by two bishops!!

Read on Missions in evening.

July, Sunday 29. 1888.

Arose early. Pleasant weather. Attended service in A.M. Sermon by Rev. De Jong. Enjoyed a season of Prayer at noon.

Addressed church at Englewood in behalf of Foreign Missions on Hand. 16:9 Good audience & was greatly helped in speaking. Sold map to S.S. (?) Mr. Kempers took me with Buggy to Roneland. Addressed 600 people in evening. Was helped again in answer to prayer. Rev. Van den Berg[17] was present & also Rev. Van Ess. The latter addressed the meeting after we left the pulpit.

Retired at 10.30

July, Monday 30. 1888.

Arose at 7.00 Spent A.M. in letter writing & reading. P.M. ditto. Took train at 6 P.M. for South Holland. Was cordially received by Rev. Van Houten [Van Houte][18] & lodged at A. Gowens Heavy thunder shower in A.M.

Albert Vanden Berg (1860-1924), WTS, 1888, Pastor, Newkirk, IA, 1888-91. HD, 407
[18]   Jacob Van Houte (1845-1919), Pastor, South Holland, IL, 1886-91. HD, 427

July, Tuesday 31. 1888.

Breakfast. Walked to Depot — Ticket for Chicago. Went to Laundry etc – Registered at Globe European Hotel State St. – Very Good. Put on clean clothes & feel like a new man. Travel — is detrimental to cleanliness! Called at R.R. Offices & obtained ½ fare passes as engaged in Missy-work for the summer.

Attended Noonday Prayer-Meeting.

P.M. in sight-seeing. Visited Museum of Anatomy.

Spent evening at Hotel Room 14 writing & reading.

August 1888

August, Wednesday 1. 1888.

Arose early. Wrote letters & sent letter with article on Missions & Missy Plate to "De Hope"

Took train at 4.45 P.M. for Irving Park after having obtained a half fare pass on the North Western R.R. Was met at Depot by Rev. Phraner[1].

Pleasant stay. Olive Phraner is very entertaining for a four year old. Addressed meeting in evening.

Quite good attendance. Mr. Cushing gave me $2.00 to-day for a Missy. Map.

Accepted with Thanks. Retired late. Good quarters.

August, Thursday 2. 1888.

Arose at 7 A.M.

Wrote letters to A.B. Reed etc & saw the village. Dinner at the Parsonage. Took 1 P.M. train for Chicago "Bus" for downtown".

Met Mr. P. Sinclair again & visited Farwell Hall.

Street Car for 418 Harrison St. Rev. De Bey's Not very hospitable reception. Family not "home"-like.

Heavy thunder-storm. Spoke in evening — audience small — But "godliness <u>with</u> contentment" is great gain even if I slept in a bed 3x5 ft & in a damp room – terrible for health.

August, Friday 3. 1888.

Arose early (!) [see yesterday's entry] Who could sleep long in a steam chest?

Breakfast (!) Visited Mr. Luxen's Dutch School.

Train at 11 A.M. for South Holland. Walked from depot. Walked to Joh. Ravensloot in P.M. with a son of Rev. Van Houten.

Kind reception. Grietge is as ever.

Mr. R. took us to church with buggy. Rain again but quite good attendance. Spoke on Missions. & was helped in my delivery.

Fell happy & experienced the power of prayer. Slept at Gowen's.

[1]   William Henry Phraner (1841-1912), Pastor, Irving Park, Chicago, IL. 1883-1888. HD, 307

♪

August, Saturday 4. 1888.

Train at 5:37 A.M. for Chicago. Received Laundry. Train at 8 A.M. for Milwaukee to Rev. Jno. Broek. Dinner. Received mail; quite a treat to a traveling drummer.

After dinner took train for Franklin via Oakwood. Was dissappointed Mr. - & Martina Kotr's were at depot but he said he could not possibly take me to Milwaukee on Sunday! Broek to speak there in evening I had to decline Franklin & went back to M. on 5.30 Train. Met drummer to-day for whom I promised to pray _ Mr. A. Werner.

Retired late; Mr. Anvelink

♪

August, Sunday 5. 1888.

Arose early: Am lodged into Mr. Mentingh. Heard Sermon in A.M. by John Broek Good. Studied in A.M. on sermon.

Preached for Rev. John Broek from Math: - Large attendance. Called at parsonage & took supper.

Missy. Address in evening on Rev. 3:8. Large number of young people.

Received two answers to prayer to-day. Thank God.

Met Mrs. Huntkanf & Mr. & Mrs. Knoes.

♪

August, Monday 6. 1888.

Arose at 7.00 Spent A.M. in writing & making appointments ahead for next week.

Walk down town & received half – fare permits on two R.R's.

Dinner at Drappers.

Called at A. Geerlings Harrison St.

Car for 673 11th Street . Supper & pleasant social hour at Albert Knoes. Mrs. Knoes is as pleasant as ever. Such a home proves the truth of all the write sayings in regard to it.

Retired late —

tired out with the rush of the day.

%

August, Tuesday 7. 1888.

Arose early. Called at Knoes. Fixed Gate & Mrs. <u>Panels</u> mended my coat.

Took train at 11 A.M. for Cedar Grove.

Dinner & good fare at Rev. Stapelkamp's[2]. Spent P.M. in a drive to Mr. Harmeling[3]. Played croquet.

Supper at Rev. Stapk [Staplekamp]. Addressed large audience in evening (@ 475). Was helped in speaking in answer to prayer.

Took train, after a cup of milk at 10.30 for Milwaukee.
Street-car & walk to Mr. <u>Mertagh</u>.

Tired & worn-out.

%

August, Wednesday 8. 1888.

Arose at 6 A.M. breakfast & car for <u>C.M.</u> & St. Paul Depot. Train for Waupun Met at depot by Rev. Sherman.

Dinner. Waupun is building a new church. Had hair-cut & bought pair of cuff-buttons. As I lost mine en route. Addressed church in evening on request

Visited State Prison in P.M. Quite an <u>instructive</u> sight.

They are engaged in making new soles (!) good work for convicts.

Large audience in evening.
Rode to <u>Alto</u> with Mr. Druer.

Retired.

%

August, Thursday 9. 1888.

Spent Morning at Mr. Druer's. Rode around country & met several of the farmers.

Met "neef John"[4] & visited his blacksmith-shop.

[2] Evert W. Stapelkamp (1858-1908), Pastor, Cedar Grove, WI, 1888-1894. HD, 372
[3] Henry Harmeling (1864-1946), AB, Hope College, 1888. HD, 162
[4] Neef: (Dutch) Cousin

A page from Samuel's Diary.

Rainy afternoon.
Wrote letters etc.
Went to church after tea. Called at Kastein's & met Juffrouw[5] Karsten etc.

[5]   Juffrouw: (Dutch) Miss

Addressed meeting in church on "The Subject of xtiany."

Large attendance. Rev. Te Winkel [Te Winkle][6] being absent I conducted all the services.

After service Martin Druer drove me to Waupun & thence I took stage for Chester.

Train at 1:30 for Janesville Jction.

♃

August, Friday 10. 1888.

Slept in "caboose" quite well (the cushioned seats were too short for my long limbs) Interesting talk with Brakeman[7].

Breakfast at Janesville — 20 minutes.

Train for Chicago. Read book of Revelation on train. Arrived at C. 10:20. Called on Mr. P. St. Clair. Received some interesting information. was asked to write for "Rec. v [of] xtian Work" accepted, Mr. P. St. Clair gave me some interesting leaflets (400) for use this summer. Left Chicago at 12 M. Met Prof. Ftoam[overwritten with Straw][8] of Wheaton on board train. —

Arrived at Fulton Ills. at 4:58 P.M.

Brother Adrian[9] met me at Depot (!) He is here on land — agency business.

♃

August, Saturday 11. 1888.

The entries previous

to Saturday the

11th up to Tuesday
are one <u>day back</u>.

♃

6 John William Te Winkle (1836-1901), Pastor, Alto, WI, 1886-1888. HD, 393
7 Brakeman: A crewmember often assigned to the caboose of a train to assist with braking. Michigan Central Railroad Company. *Rules for the Government of the Conducting Transportation Department*, The W.S. Gilkey Printing Co, Cleveland, Ohio, 1916.
8 Darien A. Straw (1857-1950), M.S. Principal of Wheaton Preparatory School and Professor of Logic and Rhetoric. WC, 5
9 Adrian Peter Zwemer (1861-1895), brother of Samuel Zwemer. MH; https://www.findagrave.com/memorial/135552242/adrian-p-zwemer

August, Sunday 12. 1888.

Preached in A.M. for Fulton Church. Math 19:26.

Large attendance & good church building. —

Am staying with Mr. G. De Bey[10] — pleasant place.

Preached Missy. sermon in P.M. but was not allowed to hang up my chart _ as it was Sunday(!) A singing — school was held in same building after the service by the young people (!!) "Consistency thou art a jewel".

After tea I led the prayer-meeting (services all day in Holland) Ps. 130.

Heard Presb. Minister in evening.

Blessed & happy day. Retired at 9:30.

August, Monday 13. 1888.

Arose at 2:30 A.M. train for Ames Iowa.

Feel sleepy. Breakfast at Cedar Rapids.

Met Ex. Gov. St. John[11] on train & had pleasant conversation on Politics & the third party vote.

Changed cars at Ames. Arrived at Des Moines at 1.30 P.M. Stopped at the Aborn House[12]. (Good place) Visited capitol building etc. Saw. "James Aldrich Collection of autographs & photos" very fine. & worth a visit to the capitol.

Supper. Attended Prohibition meeting & heard Ex. Gov. St. John. Very good speaker & convincing.

Am I a Prohibitionist?

St. John treated me on Soda Water after lecture (!)

August, Tuesday 14. 1888.

Good night's rest. Called by Porter at 5 A.M.

Dressed & washed — train on C.R. Island & Pac. for Pella, Iowa.

Bus for Rev. Moerdyke. Kind reception & good breakfast. Quite different from that of Rev. De Bey at Chicago.

[10] George De Bey (1848-1920), Owner, General Store, Fulton, WI. Portraitbiogra1885 DeBay.pdf, 646. *Portrait and Biographical Album of Whiteside County, Illinois.* Chicago, 1885, 646.
[11] John Pierce St. John (1833-1916), Governor of Kansas, 1879-1883. *Britannica* 15th Ed. v10, 321
[12] Aborn House was an inn located in Des Moines, Iowa.

Heavy rain-storm to-day. Spent day "at home" writing & reading.
Called on Rev. Smit[13] & Rev. Sharpley[14] & made appointment for next sabbath.

§

August, Wednesday 15. 1888.

Attended Prayer Meeting this evening & led in request Ps. 130. —

For the rest spent day very pleasantly with Rev. Moerdyke in studying at Exegesis. We made two sermon sketches.
{Jno. 12:22
{Math 17:24 – 27

Each selecting one text.

Pleasant & profitable day.

§

August, Thursday 16. 1888.

Attended Picnic of Young People 1st Ref. Church.

Quite a good time — Weller's Grove. 37 present. Games etc.
Had the Misfortune to break three saucers! Pleasant drive home.
Read & Wrote letters.

§

August, Friday 17. 1888.

Attended Missy. Picnic on invitation of Rev. Sharpley. About 150 children belonging to Mission Circle -- met at Big Rock — 2 ½ miles from Pella. A rock — perhaps a meteor-stone — 12x22x12 ft near a creek.
Pleasant time.
Gave short Missy. address with maps etc in P.M. to children.

Rode home with Mrs. Van. Buskirk.
Wrote letters to James Van Hoven & Mrs. Van der Meide in regard to Missions.
Wrote article for "De Hope" Received letter from Rev. Van Houten

[13] John Smit (1842-1911), Pastor, Third Reformed Church, Pella, IA. 1886-91. HD, 364
[14] George Sharpley (?-?), Pastor, Second, Pella. 1887-92. HD, 357

South Holland Ill.

Saturday in visiting.

§

Sunday August, ~~Saturday~~ 18. 19 1888.[15]

Spoke in 3rd Ref. Ch. at Pella in A.M. Rev. Smit is not in favor of Missions. He combats man's free-will so as to include the purse in predestination! Spoke in 1st Ref. Ch. in P.M. 900 present. Rev. Moerdyke's prayer was an inspiration. Was greatly helped in speaking. Addressed Ladies Meeting & received Pledge for $60 for 5 years in support of a Missionary.

Supper at Moerdykes.

Spoke in 2nd Ref. Ch. in evening. Quite a number present. Special Collection. Met Rev. Zigler[16] etc. Altogether a day of blessing. I trust all my sabbaths may be as happy in service.

§

August, Sunday 19. 1888.

[No Entry]

§

August, Monday 20. 1888.

Arose early. Spent day in helping with wash etc. Called on Elder Breen. Received $10 from an unknown donor for Missions.

Called on Mrs. Vander Zijl etc.

Supper with Moerdyke's at Welle's. Miss. K. Welle. & her sister are good at conversation.

Left Wells at 10 P.M. Played checkers & talked with Mr. & Mrs. Moerdyke until 1 A.M. then took "bus" for depot.

Ticket for Des Moines where I arrived at 3 A.M.

Slept in Rock Island Depot until day — light —

§

---

[15] Day Crossed out and date overwritten with 19.
[16] A.G. Ziegler (1833-1915), Pastor, Bethel, Pella, IA, 1887-1892. HD, 479

August, Tuesday 21. 1888.

Walked through Des Moines. Fire & Explosion on Walnut Street! Bought spade for Johmie Train on N.W.R.R. at 9:50 A.M. for Orange City.

Took dinner at Eagle Grove.

The N.W.R.R. goes through more romantic but not more fertile country – than the C.M. & St. Paul. Arrived at Alton at 6 P.M. James told me Father was there so I got my baggage & left train.

Supper at Kate's. All well & glad to see me.

Spent evening in small talk about plans etc past & future.

Am tired of travelling.

♇

August, Wednesday 22. 1888.

Spent A.M. in garden with brother Jas. F. Zwemer. He has accepted the appointment to act as financial agent for the Western Institutions of our Church.

P.M. ditto.

Drove to Alton with Maud. Received Mail & called on Rev. Buursma[17] & Rev. De Spelder[18].

Made appointment for next sunday.

Supper at Jas. F.

Drove home with Father. Left coat at tailors for repairs.

Read & Studied.

♇

August, Thursday 23. 1888.

Walked to & fro through the length & breadth of Father's possessions!

One indeed feels "out doors" on the Prairies.

Made catch on Barn — doors & a Carpenter's bench for Father.

[17]   Ale. Buursma (1841-1901), Pastor, Orange City, IA, 1879-89. HD, 60

[18]   John A. De Spelder (1851-1914), Pastor, American, Orange City, IA, 1887-94. HD, 100

Spent Afternoon in writing letters to a dozen neglected correspondents.

Also sent away 40 copies of "Hoe Hindu Christienen" geven"[19] translated by me from the Dutch.

Evening at home; helped pickling beans etc.

August, Friday 24. 1888.

Went to Orange City in A.M. with ~~Fathers~~ horse. of Mr. Kloek on business. Called in P.M. on Rev. De Pree, Sioux Centre for making an appointment. Met Mr. Waarenberg's father. He is sorry his son did not go to the Foreign Field.

Is the Western Seminary to blame? —?

Why do people dissuade those who have once decided to go?

Spent evening after drive at home.

August, Saturday 25. 1888.

Spent A.M. in Study & letter writing.

Wrote to Miss. A. Skillman in reference to speaking for their Y.P.U. on Missions at Chicago.

Drove to Orange City with Maud & thence took train for Alton where I staid with Sister Kate. Evening at home _ amusing my nieces with puzzle games etc.

Feel very tired & not in the right mood to speak to-morrow, but I trust I shall received the right mood as well as the right Spirit in season. God never gives his blessing before we <u>need</u> it.

August, Sunday 26. 1888.

Arose early. Attended to horse & buggy.

Spoke in Alton church in A.M. on Foreign Missions Large audience & appreciative. Received the approval of sister Kate & the consistory.

---

[19]   Hoe Hindu Christienen geven: (Dutch) How Hindu Christians give.

Rode to Orange City with D. Gleysteen[20].
Spoke in 1st Ref. Church. Large audience & good attention.
Spoke to S.S. & raised $243 as test – not pledged for certain.
Supper at Rev. De Spelder. Spoke in 2d Ref. Ch. in Evening. Good attendance. Very warm on stage _ They have as yet no church building & hold their meetings in a theatre. Drove back to Alton.

9

August, Monday 27. 1888.

A.M. at home with Sister Kate.
Took the girls out for a drive in P.M.
Train at 6.30 for Orange City.
Met Ladies Missy. Society in evening.
$60 pledged for 5 years!

Good results.

Remained over night at Buursma's.

Rev. B. is social & not "ultra" in his opinions. Talked Politics & the 3d Party Movement.

9

August, Tuesday 28. 1888.

Train at 900 for Alton _ Freight – train.
Drove from Alton to Free Grace Parsonage. After dinner came back with Sister Nellie.
Pleasant call at Schallekanks.
Drove to Alton again.
Supper at Kate's.
Invited to spend evening with Gleysteen's.
Pleasant time.
Miss. Cynthia G.[21] (Adrian's intended) is a fine girl. She was a great deal of character & is not superficial.

---

[20] Likely Dirk Vanderlinden Gleysteen (1870-1951), brother of Klazina (Cynthia) Gleysteen, Adrian Zwemer's fiancee. https://www.findagrave.com/memorial/135550796/dirk-vander_linden-gleysteen
[21] Klazina (also known as: Zina, Sientje, Cynthia) Gleysteen Zwemer (1868-1947), Adrian Zwemer's fiancee and later second wife.https://www.findagrave.com/memorial/135552262/klazina-sientje-zwemer

Nellie Zwemer

Retired at 1 A.M.

℘

August, Wednesday 29. 1888.

Arose at 6.00 Drove to Orange City & thence with Nellie home.

Read & Studied. Wrote article for Press "Record of Xtian Work" entitled : "The Foreign Missy outlook at home"

A Party of young people from Orange City called in Evening. Mr. H. Hospers[22] with seven ladies! & that for supper at 7 P.M.

Some people always look at hospitality subjectively!

℘

August, Thursday 30. 1888.

Arose late. Tended to horses etc.
Read & amused little Johnnie.
Drove to Newkirk with sister Nellie in 40 min 8 miles. Pleasant day for drive.
Dinner at Rev. V. d. Berg. Rev. & Mrs. De Spelder called there also & drove home with us.

[22]   Likely Henry Hospers (1869-1937), Free U, Amsterdam, 1889-1890. HD, 186

Supper.
A large gathering of the youth of our church.

Singing etc.

What is so wearying & wearing as three evening parties in succession?

$$\mathcal{Z}$$

August, Friday 31. 1888.

Spent A.M. at home. went to Mr. — for some oats etc.
Drove to Orange City in P.M. for mail.

Received letter from A. Pieters[23] & postal from I. Vernon.
Spent evening in reading & writing for Press.

---

[23]   Albertus Pieters (1869-1955), AM, Hope College, 1890. HD, 308

September 1888

September, Sunday 1. 1888.

Spent A.M. at home & in helping sisters cut & can corn for winter. Read Missy Review of the world for Sept.

Went to Alton with father in evening & thence after meeting James F. with train to Maurice.
Cordial reception at Rev. H.K. Boer[1].
Supper & retired early.

Will have a busy day to-morrow.

$$\mathcal{2}$$

September, Sunday 2. 1888.

Arose at 6:30 A.M. Read Hewbrew Bible. Breakfast. Rehearsed my speech & hung up Missy. maps in church. Addressed about 200 in A.M. Very attentive. Mr. Durer drove me to Sioux Centre (7 miles[overwritten on 10]) & I there supplied pulpit for Rev. De Pree. About 600 present.
Good attention & a great deal of sympathy expressed for the cause after the service. Mr. Harmelink took me to Alton with horse & buggy. Was helped all day in my work greatly — but was not as thankful or spiritual as I should be . "Oh for a closer walk with God".

$$\mathcal{2}$$

September, Monday 3. 1888.

Arose at 2 A.M. & took train at 3 [A.M.] for Sioux City. Saw Corn Palace & other sights. Sioux City is a bustling active town for its size.
Train at 8:30 for Tripp Dakota. Dinner at Scotland. Tripp has 4 saloons & no evangelical church. Pop. about 400. From Tripp to Armour. Brother Fred. J. Met us at armour & we drove with his "Gospel — team" of Wild ponies to Grand View.
Supper at Hotel.
Pleasant Conversation in evening.
Fred's bachelor-quarters are very good.
Gd. View the typical western town was moved on wheels two years ago.

$$\mathcal{2}$$

---

[1]   Henry K. Boer (1845-1919), Pastor, Maurice, IA, 1885-90. HD, 35

September, Tuesday 4. 1888.

Spent day in visiting in & around Grand View. Drove to school house, Mr. Brown, etc etc, Mr. Bÿl where we took tea... thence to Rev. Stegeman[2] at Harrison.

Spoke on Missions in evening

Large audience for Harrison.

Mr. J.J. Gregory M.D. called in evening. He volunteered to go to the foreign field!!

Lively conversation & pleasant entertainment.

Slept at Stegeman's.

෭

September, Wednesday 5. 1888.

Breakfast. Sketched Parsonage & church. Wrote letters.

Drove in company with F.J. & Maud with Miss. Linda Van Eyck to White Swan — 30 miles — Fine view of Indian Reservation. White Swan is an Indian Post Office & interesting. Crossed the Muddy Missouri & visited Ft. Randall — 400 soldiers — pay-day when we visited. Cannon & officers quarters.

Drove back along Govt. Dug-Ways to Indian Agency at Greenwood Yankton Sioux Reservation. Supper at Indian Mess- house...!

Bad night on account of bed- bugs & vermin. Log-house hospitality!

෭

September, Thursday 6. 1888.

Arose early! Or rather did not sleep all night. Fed horses.

Visited Indian Mission Schools ... St. Paul; Govt; & Presbyterian ...

Miss Bates at St. Paul school is fine teacher. Bought Moccasins, pipe & war club at Indian agency.

Drive back to Armour. Improvised dinner.

Back to Grand View.

Rev. Stegeman called. Heavy thunder-shower but still had a meeting in behalf of For. Missions.

20 present!

---

[2]   Abraham Stegeman (1857-1899), Pastor, Harrison, SD, 1883-1892. HD, 374

Spoke 15 min. & then ceased on account v [of] shower.
Slept with Rev. Stegeman on sofa.

§

September, Friday 7. 1888.

Arose at 7.30 A.M.
Am rested & feel very well this A.M.
Breakfast at Hotel.
Drive in great haste to Armour. Just in time for train. Arrived at Tripp 12.55. Dinner at Hotel. Arrived at Sioux City 6.05 P.M. Saw famous corn-Palace & heard choir practice for Festival week.
Y.M.C.A. Rooms also were visited. Has 400 members. 7 Hollanders also active members. Walk to Depot.
Helped lady to a Hotel who was lost.
Train at 10.50 for Alton arrived at 12.50.
Slept with Brother Adrian at Jame's.

Feel tired.

§

September, Saturday 8. 1888.

Packed trunk in A.M. Went home via Orange City.
Studied & read in afternoon & evening.

Nellie & I had some good heart – talks during vacation & I trust she has consecrated herself to the Foreign work.

§

September, Sunday 9. 1888.

Arose early. Drove to Newkirk 7 miles. Broke buggy a mile from home but repaired with strap. Addressed large audience on Missions; much interest. I was greatly helped in speaking. How much greater is God's love than our faith in that love! After dinner drove home & spoke to Father's church in P.M. Crowded. Many sat in wagons drawn alongside the church.
Was again helped. Met young people in S.S. & raised $36.00 in yearly pledges.

Drove with Father to Alton where I leave to-morrow for the East. What a blessed day this has been.

§

September, Monday 10. 1888.

Arose early. Took broken buggy to blacksmith. Sent trunk to depot. Took train at 9.40 for Wheaton Ills.

Many ministers on board as they go to Classis at Pella. Good lunch. From Jewell Junction Mr. Gleysteen & I travelled alone.

At Eagle Grove a party of Cornell Students joined us & we sang gospel hymns etc until Midnight when they left us. Met one of the volunteers. I trust we shall all once meet when the work is done. Slept very poorly in a crowded train.

§

September, Tuesday 11. 1888.

Arrived at Wheaton Ills. at 6.30 Breakfast in a Restaurant.

Met Prof. Straw & Mr. Fifield & made arrangements to address students in evening on For. Missions. Felt very weak spiritually but prayer was strengthening & after tea I went to chapel. About 70 students present. Spoke for @ 30 minutes & then passed volunteer — Pledge. 13 new ones confirmed themselves willing & desirous to go out as Foreign Missionaries!

Praise God for so honoring me as his instrument.

Retired very happy — but not thankful enough.

§

September, Wednesday 12. 1888.

Breakfast at Prof Straw's. Took train at 7.55 for Chicago.

Went to Y.M.C.A. Rooms. Stored trunk with Messrs Kelder & Eimers S. Water Street.

Received Mail & then went to Mr. Vernon. Sorry to hear that engagement was cancelled. But all is for the best.

Supper at Vernon's. Attended Park Congl. Church Prayer-Meeting. An (odinc) comparison was made at the meeting between the benevolence v [of] the church & Masonic- fraternity! "Whatever is, is (not) right" Retired feeling little desire to pray. How cold hearted we are!

♫

September, Thursday 13. 1888.

Arose early. Breakfast with the Vernon's.

Went down town to do business. Tried to get reduction in fares but did not succeed very well.

Attended Noon -day meet in Farwell Hall & was greatly blessed. Spent P.M. in seeing city. Called on several parties with Mr. Pieter Sinclair.

Was asked to attend Youth Meeting on South Side in evening. Did so. Mr. Smith led. Many anxious ones! Oh the vast need of reaching the masses! When will churches & pastors be filled with the Missy spirit. Had sweet talk with a Catholic enquirer, who felt the need v [of] a Savior.

♫

September, Friday 14. 1888.

Arose early & met Father at train. Breakfast at a Restaurant.

Sightseeing all morning. Eden Musée[3] etc.

Went to bid farewell to the Vernons & to thank them for all their kindness. Met students at Congl. Theol. Sem. as per appointment & spoke on Missions. 15 new volunteers! Thank God. Received a greeting for New Brunswick by a rising vote.

Went in haste to Boat Landing & took Boat for Gd. Haven. Father & I had State-room no. 31. Wrote letters. Pleasant night & no sea-sickness.

♫

September, Saturday 15. 1888.

Arrived at Gd. Haven at 5:30 A.M. Walked to Ed. Hofna M. D. Hearty reception & a warm breakfast atoned for all the inconvenience of travel. Father went on to Holland. Drove to Spring Lake; dinner at Mulders & talk on Relative needs v [of] Home & For. Missions.

Drove back per. Spent P.M. in writing letters etc. Evening at home with Doctor & wife.

[3] Eden Musée was an entertainment venue in New York City opened in 1884. http://daytoninmanhattan.blogspot.com/2010/12/lost-eden-musee-wonders-of-world-in-wax.html

Read (Book on Somnambulism[4] – Very good & scientific only too apt to sneer at Revelation.

Retired, praying for help for busy day tomorrow.

ℰ

September, Sunday 16. 1888.

Arose early. Studied morning discourse. Went to church in company with Elder Mul.

Very rainy but good attendance. Spoke with some grace on Math — "If any man will come after me".

Addressed S.S. on Missions & held their attention to the end.

Preached Missy. sermon. in P.M. Very much helped by Spirit to make an earnest plea. After meeting spoke with Ladies v [of] Missy Soc. They promised to do more than ever - - -. Supper at Juisterna's. Met J. Luxen etc. Took Boat at 6 P.M. for Chicago so as to make connections.

ℰ

September, Monday 17. 1888.

Spent A.M. in rainy, wet & dirty Chicago.

Bought ticket via Niagara Short Line & received a reduction of 75 cents.

Transferred trunk etc. Pleasant ride through Illinois & Michigan. Met a Canadian on the train at Detroit & spoke of our national relations & the Retaliation Bill[5] passed by the House. All our baggage was examined at Detroit by the Customs House Officials.

The ride was over a roughly laid road & not very agreeable. Did not sleep very much.

ℰ

September, Tuesday 18. 1888.

Arrived at Niagara Falls about 8 A.M. Took Cars for Falls. Did not meet P.J.Z. Saw all the grandeur of this Master piece of the Creator.

Went to Goat Island Luna Island. Sisters etc etc. & took ride

4   Somnambulism: Sleepwalking
5   Canadian Retaliation Bill passed by the House of Representatives (176-4) September 8, 1888. Benson John Lossing, Woodrow Wilson, *Harper's Encyclopaedia of United States History from 458 A.D. to 1912*, Volume 9, Harper & Brothers Publishers, New York and London, 1912.

Edward Tanjore Corwin

in Maid of the Mist under the spray! Read the 104th Ps. aloud on the Canada side & never before saw so much beauty in it.

Left Niagara at 3:40 P.M. & took Erie for New York.

Disagreeable ride in a packed train.

♂

September, Wednesday 19. 1888.

Changed Cars at Buffalo & again at Hornersville[6]. Arrived at Jersey City (two hrs late) at 9 A.M. Transferred trunk for which a Mr. Sherry – Expressman – charged me the small sum of 75 cents!! Took train at 11:25 for New Brunswick.

Met all the boys. _ Happy reunion.

The new Rector Dr. Corwin[7] is very social & kind.

Heard opening address by Dr. Demarest in evening; quite strong. New class numbers 17.

Am now in Room No 40. Very pleasant quarters.

Retired early.

♂

[6]   Likely Hornellsville, NY.

[7]   Edward Tanjore Corwin (1834-1914), Pastor, Hillsborough, Millstone, NJ, 1863-1888, Rector, Instructor, New Brunswick Theological Seminary 1888-95. HD, 79

September, Thursday 20. 1888.

Arose late & still feel tired of travel; Attended Recitations & heard preliminaries Spent rest of time in arranging my room.

Bought Rug for $6.50

Spent evening in reading & writing.
Read 43 pgs. in Hodge for Dr. Mabon.
Enjoyed a brief season of prayer.

September, Friday 21. 1888.

Arose early. Breakfast. Attended all recitations. Have resolved to spend one hour each day (as last year) from 12 – 1 P.M. in prayer & Bible Reading.

Dr. Mabon was very good this morning ; he awakens a desire for study & original investigation.
Spent P.M. in writing & reading.
Helped Mr. Bomben[8] a German student to study English.
Read & sent out Missy literature this evening.
Feel tired & a little unwell.
Hope to go to New York to-morrow.

September, Saturday 22. 1888.

Arose at 6 A.M. Train for New York. Called on Intelligencer Office & settled accounts. Called on Dr. Cobb & received Balance of $75 for payment in part of Expenses for summer work.

Feel quite well satisfied Although I have worked very hard for so little pay.

Visited Union Seminary. Purchased Gray's Bib Museum (10 vols) $8.00 a Fine set.

Called on Dr. Mabon & Dr. Corwin in evening & had a most pleasant time. Read Bible & Retired. Feel ^somewhat unsatisfied with myself & the world.

[8]   John Bombin (1858-1931), New Brunswick Theological Seminary, 1891. HD, 38

William Augustus
Van Vranken Mabon

September, Sunday 23. 1888.

Arose early. Pleasant season of prayer with the boys after break-fast. Attended Regular service at Dr. Campbells. Good Practical sermon on Gal. 6:10 Was welcomed back to my old church home. Attended S.S. in P.M.

Pleasant hour with my old class of 6 girls.

Heard Missy Stout (Japan) in P.M. Good but lacking in fire. A Grand subject such as Missions agent to fire every man especially a Missionary. Evening Prayers were good subject, Love of God.

Went to Throop Ave. Mission Spoke on P<u>rayer</u> & its <u>Need</u>. Was greatly blessed. Two asked for Prayers in their own behalf.

September, Monday 24. 1888.

Arose at 7 A.M. Spent A.M. in writing & study.

Sent a circular letter on Missions to 52 Western Pastors. Trust it may awaken some interest. Attended Recitations – but made a failure (the whole class did) in Dr. Mabon's Room.

Studied & Read Hebrew Bible in evening.

Wrote letters to J.M. Allen & "Gospel in All Lands" etc.

Mr. Keeling & Andrew called during the day. Mr. Mc Afee (M.E.

Ch.) asked me to secure two Missy speakers for Oct. 7th in their church. Will do so.

♪

September, Tuesday 25. 1888.

Attended Recitations in A.M. Pleasant hours. Enjoyed noon-day hour of Prayer exceedingly. "Ah how sweet is the hour of prayer!"
Spent P.M. in reading Hodge & study.
Must arrange for meeting of mission band soon.

Had a call from Miss. Corwin in my room. Pleasant Conversationist. Read & wrote article on Turkey & Robert's College for De Hope. Read Bible. Retired late.

♪

September, Wednesday 26. 1888.

Attended Recitations. This evening first Meeting of Society of Inquiry.

Am now elected to act as Treasurer.

Our Prayer-meeting today was very well attended & a good spirit prevailed.

♪

September, Thursday 27. 1888.

Attended all Recitations. Read & studied all day.

Called on Dr. Woodbridge in evening & gave him Hist & Missions to review.
I hope he will introduce it as a text- book.
Read Bible as usual & retired.

♪

September, Friday 28. 1888.

Attended all recita's except Dr. De Witt's.
Took train for New York at 12:55 P.M.

Visited Synod's Rooms etc. Went to Union College & met R.P. Wilder.

Had a most pleasant season of refreshing with him in conversation & prayer.

He expects to spend this year in work among the colleges.

Met J.O. Stoops. Asked him to address the students here next Sabbath.

Supper at Restaurant & late train home.
Wrote until 12 M & retired.

$$\wr$$

September, Saturday 29. 1888.

Arose early. Breakfast. Selected sermon & Missionary address for Marlborough Ch.

Took train at 12:33 for Monmouth Jc. thence to Freehold & thence to Wickatunk.

Was met at the depot by three little daughters of Mr. Van Kirk.
Pleasant place to stay.

Grandmother Van kirk is a praying Xtian & lives near to Christ. Mr. V. K has 123 acres of good land & the whole family seem happy.

Music & conversation in evening.

$$\wr$$

September, Sunday 30. 1888.

Arose at 6.30. Read over Scripture & Sermon Drove to old Brick Church _ 60 years old congregation more than 125 years standing. About 150 present.

Text I Cor. 15:58.

Very cold in church. but my heart grew warm under my subject.

Oh that we could have greater consecrat & more activity in the Xtian life. of to-day.

October 1888

October, Monday 1. 1888.

Left Freehold early & arrived at New Brunswick about 10 A.M. Attended Recitations in P.M.

October, Tuesday 2. 1888.

Attended all Recitations as usual.

Mission Circle met in my room for 1ˢᵗ time this year.
Dr. Lansing present.

Good hour & profitably spent.
Called on Mrs. Peeke in evening with Beardslee Pleasant time of social pleasure.
Recd. Letter from A.B.R. & from Sister Nellie.

October, Wednesday 3. 1888.

Attended Recitations
The first prayer-meeting led by Mr. Adams[1] was good & inspiring. Very pleasant hour. Asked prayers for Chas. Thew & wrote him a letter this evening.

October, Thursday 4. 1888.

Attended Recitations
Studied —
Enjoyed a season of prayer this noon at regular place & time.

October, Friday 5. 1888.

Attended Recitations Spent P.M. in reading & writing for the Press.
Received a call from Mr. Mcgee M.E. Church who asked me to speak for them on Missions next Sab. Consented.

[1] William Ten Eyck Adams (1863-1936), New Brunswick Theological Seminary, 1891. HD, 2

Social of Y.P.U. at Dr. Demarest's this evening. As good a time as one generally has at such gatherings. Miss. Aiken recited for us.

Walked home with Miss. Christopher.

October, Sunday 6. 1888.

Spent day in study. Read Book of Esther etc.
Prepared speech for M.E. Church & wrote letters.

Called on Doolittle's Pleasant time with Mrs. D.
Went to Depot for Mr. Stoops. Had a blessed season of prayer before we retired.
He is from Union Sem. & will speak at M.E. Church to-morrow.

Slept in Tilton's Room.

October, Sunday 7. 1888.

Attended Prayer Meeting held in my room. 7 present. Was blessed. Went to 1st M.E. Church with Mr. Stoops — Communion service. Very impressive! All are one in Christ.
Dinner. Attended S.S. at Suydam St. & taught my class.
Church service Dr. Campbell — Col 3:1 —
Resurrection of Christ. Waked home with Miss. Corwin & had a pleasant talk on Xtian Growth. Went to Chapel service in evening Mr. Stoops spoke on Missions. 2 new volunteers.
Went to M.E. Church & was greatly helped in my addressing the people. Thanked God & retired.

October, Monday 8. 1888.

Arose early. Breakfast. Walked to Depot with brother Stoops.
Studied Hebrew etc. Read about Materialism etc. in Hodge — How Blessed is the Bible — above all scientific theories!
Attended Recitations. Spent evening in Study & writing letters. May God help me to live as Zinzendorf[2] did & rather be hated for Jesus sake than loved for my own even when I meet with scoffs and jeers.

[2]   Christian Renatus von Zinzendorf - or Nikolaus Ludwig, Graf von Zinzendorf 1700-1760. leader of the Moravian Church. *Britannica* 15th Ed. v12, 921

$$\mathcal{G}$$

October, Tuesday 9. 1888.

Arose early. Attended all recitations. Had a call from Mr. Strong[3] Princeton '91 who desires me to teach him French for a month. Accepted on 90 cents an ~~minu~~ hour.

Mission Circle met this afternoon. Rev. Stout was present. He spoke very earnestly on the work in Japan but somewhat desparingly of the Volunteer Movement.

Of course the o-missy fellows used this as a cudgel to hit all Foreign Missy cranks.

Well if God leads the movement why should we fear or be dismayed. He can make the wrath of men to praise him.

$$\mathcal{G}$$

October, Wednesday 10. 1888.

Attended Recitations Spent an hour with Mr. Strong & this was unfortunate in losing the prayer-meeting.

Spent P.M. in study & writing.
Took Dutch tract to Printer & it will be ready for Proof – reading on Tuesday next.

Spent evening in trying to write a college song – with small success. Will have to try again.

Am not in a poetic mood at present & the muse seems to fear Theological Sanctions & Dry-as-dust Investigations.

$$\mathcal{G}$$

October, Thursday 11. 1888.

Attended all Recitations. Recd. letter from Kingston church asking for me on Sun. the 21st.
Taught Mr. Strong from 12 – 1 P.M.

Spent P.M. in Study. Bought Mc Clintock & Strong's Encyclopedia 12 wks for $48 on special reduction. Am to pay $10 down &

---

[3]   Robert Boorman Strong (1871-1904), Princeton College, 1891. Princeton, 157

{$10 Nov. 1ˢᵗ.
{14 Dec 1ˢᵗ in _full._
{14 Jan 1ˢᵗ

Was greatly in need of something of the kind. Had a call from George & James Mabon this evening.

Read Bible & part of Tayler Lewis' Job & retired.

ℒ

October, Friday 12. 1888.

Attended Recitations. Spent afternoon in writing letters & reading.

Called on Dr. Campbell & Rev. Willis in evening. The doctor related his life history to me.
He is now 80 years old & is as hale & hearty as any young man at 20.

His life is literally one which has "abounded in every good work."
Arrived at my room at 10 P.M. read & studied.
Recd. Mc. Clintock & Strongs Encyclopedia to-day —
12 wks. — a fine set. Got them in a club at great reduction.
Retired at 12 M.

ℒ

October, Saturday 13. 1888.

Arose early. Breakfast. Wrote letters. Visited Auction store & bought some books cheap.
Wrote "Western Items" for Xtian Intelligencer for first time. Am expected to continue them weekly & to receive book in pay. Wrote letters in P.M. & drew maps & diagrams on canvas to illustrate Home Missions — talk at Kingston next Sabbath.
Called on Miss. E. Corwin in evening.
Retired late as I wrote an article for the Record of Xtian Work after 9 P.M.

ℒ

October, Sunday 14. 1888.

Prayer meeting of workers in my room this morning. A Blessing.

Barend William Lammers

Attended Suydam St. Church & heard Rev. Allan Campbell[4] on "Prayer" — Very good. Rainy & disagreeable day.

Attended S.S. & taught my class. Afternoon service Rev. A. Campbell on "Sampson". Odd sermon, but still instructive. Young People's prayer — meeting for first time. Led meeting & spoke on words: "Son go work to-day in my vineyard".

Went to Throop Ave Mission in evening & received an evening blessing.

Subject "Seeking Jesus" John 12:22.

Retired at 10.30 P.M.

❦

October, Monday 15. 1888.

Attended Recitations in P.M. Studied in Morning.

Wrote letters etc. in evening.

❦

October, Tuesday 16. 1888.

Attended Recitations. Read Proof on Dutch Missonary tract for press.

---

4   Alan D. Campbell (1844-1913), Pastor, Castleton, NY, 1882-1889. HD, 62

Mission Circle met in My room. Pleasant gathering. Home Missions the subject — Mesrrs, Cotton, & Lammers[5] the Speakers. We should not lose sight of the "beginning at Jerusalem".

Spent evening in study.

♋

October, Wednesday 17. 1888.

Attended Recitations. Studied & made some purchases in city. Bought some books at an auction hall.

♋

October, Thursday 18. 1888.

Attended Recitations — Spent P.M. in writing & reading Theology.

Went to Throop Ave in Eve. to take part in an Entertainment at the Mission. Quite a pleasant time.

Gave a "candle-talk" illustrat [pen trails off after the t] how & where to let our light shine.

Was treated to Refreshments after the exercises.

After I reached my room sat up until 1 A.M. writing addresses & sending out Sample copies of my new Missionary tract.

I trust also this effort will be owned by the Master & result in great & lasting interest in his cause among the churches v [of] 1 [the] West.

♋

October, Friday 19. 1888.

Arose early. Went to Printing Office for Miss. Leaflets _ 3000 for $8.00. Expect to sell them at 35 cts. a Hundred. Attended Recitation in Dr. Mabon's Room. Subject "Divinity v [of] Xt."

Sent out letters advertising leaflet. Read Theology.

Took train at 2.20 P.M. for New York. Call at Synod Rooms & at Dr. H.N. Cobbs. Heard the sad news of the death of Missionary Hekhuis[6]. Took Steamer Pleasant Valley for Ft. Lee. A welcome reception

5   Barend William Lammers (1860-1959), New Brunswick Theological Seminary, 1889. HD, 228

6   Lambertus Hekhuis (1849-1888), Missionary, India, 1881-88. HD, 169

at Persons. A walk in the rain — visit to Mr. Williams — chestnuts — warm fire & conversation in evening — Retired late.

§

October, Saturday 20. 1888.

Arose at 6 A.M. Breakfast. Music on Piano. —
Took ferry at 9 A.M. for 125 Street N.Y.
Cable & Elevated R.R. for Reade St. Met Mr. Phelps at 393 Pearl. Went to Medical Missy. Institute. 118 E 45th Street. Visited Broadway Tabernacle. Boat "City v [of] Kingston" for Kingston at 1 P.M. Pleasant ride up Hudson. Fine scenery — arrived at K. about 8 o'clock.

Took Cab for 220 Clinton St. & was welcomed by the Misses De Yo. where I am to stay over Sunday _

§

October, Sunday 21. 1888.

Arose at 7.30. Breakfast. Attended Services in Fair St. Ref. Ch. Good sermon by Rev. Noyes[7] on words in 2 Cor. "Unknown & yet as well known" He emphasized the importance v [of] losing sight of popularity & fame in our work for Xt.
Attended S.S. — a pleasant & lively class of little girls.
After tea called on Rev. Noyes _ Spoke in his church on <u>Home Missions</u> – illustrating my talk with maps etc.

A Good collection was taken up. I felt tired & hoarse but was helped in speaking — Oh for more more power from above to speak with power.

§

October, Monday 22. 1888.

Attended <u>Recitation</u>'s

§

7 Stephen Dutton Noyes (1841-1894), Pastor, Fair St. Kingston, NY, 1883-94. HD, 289

October, Tuesday 23. 1888.

Attended no recitation's feel sick & feverish. Recd. letter from R. Bloemendaal asking me to meet him at N.Y. took train at 5.20 P.M. Went to Brooklyn. Supper at Restaurant. — Heard Rev. Dr. Meredith in evening on S.S. Lesson.

Elevated R.R. to Gd. Union Hotel.

Slept well in Parlor "A".

♗

October, Wednesday 24. 1888.

Arose at 7.30. Breakfast. Met R. Bloem [Bloemendaal] at train. Went to Union Seminary & thence visited Bible House etc.

Took a short trip to Port Richmond & was glad again to meet Miss. H.B. Horton.

Took Bloem to Stock Exchange etc.

Steamer Bristol at 6 P.M. for Boston — May God bless the Alliance.

Pleasant time on board with — delegates of Alliance & W.C.T.U. — Song, Prayer & Speeches.

♗

October, Thursday 25. 1888.

Spent a poor night trying to sleep on floor with mattress — there being no room on Boat. Arrived at Fall River 5.30. Boston 7.00 A.M. Breakfast at Restaurant. Meeting of Welcome at 11 A.M. — nearly 500 delegates.

Had badges printed & was authorized to sell them to delegates.

Meeting in P.M. very good — Also in evening Address by Rev. J.T. Erony D.D. of Pittsburg. - in the "Crisis of the world"

Am staying at 19 St. James Ave. Very good & pleasant place for boarding

♗

October, Friday 26. 1888.

Attended meetings v [of] alliance Paper in A.M. on Japan & its crisis etc.

Led meeting for Volunteers to-day at 2:30 -

Very interesting —

All the meeting are good.

Herrick Johnson's address this evening was full of fire & fact. He said the three motives for <u>going</u> were 1. Duty 2. Compassion 3. Victory Complete.

Retired late — This is a blessed day.
Reception at Divinity School.

§

October, Saturday 27. 1888.

Attended all meety to-day. Paper on Support of a Missionary in the field especially good.

Heard several able speakers in evening. Bishop Butler – Philips Brooks[8], Dennis Osborne[9], etc.

Consecration meeting in evening. Led by R.P. Wilder.

Went to bed late – Must prepare for three services to-morrow.

Acted as chairman to day in All<u>iance</u>

§

October, Sunday 28. 1888.

Arose at 7. Breakfast. Consecration Meeting at 9. Took train (am sorry but I had to (?)) for West Newton. Spoke on Missions. Dinner at Restaurant. Attended Meet for Volunteers in P.M. then went to Y.M.C.A. & there led services. Small audience. "Prodigal Son".

Went to supper at Hall. Cars for East Boston. Addressed large audience on For. Missions. Farewell Meeting in Park Congel. Church. Grand success. —

[8]   Phillips Brooks (1835-1893), Rector, Trinity Church, Boston, MA, 1869-1891. https://en.wikipedia.org/wiki/Phillips_Brooks
[9]   Likely Rev. Dennis Osborne (1844-?), Pastor, Methodist Episcopal Church in India. Eugene R. Smith, D.D., Editor, *The Gospel in All Lands*, Hunt & Eaton, New York, 1894, 191.

James Cantine

𝄞

October, Monday 29. 1888.

Went sight seeing. Art Galleries.

Harvard College Memorial Hall Farewell.
Old State "house & New — Bunker Hill Monument — climed to top & had magnificent view of Boston Harbor.

Visited principal streets. Old South Church etc.

Took ~~boat~~ ^cars at 6.30 for Fall River Line of steamers.

Prayer Meet in Cabin with Wilder & Stoops.

Blessed time.

𝄞

October, Tuesday 30. 1888.

Arrived at New York 8:30 Escorted a stranger (lady) to New Brunswick.
Attended no Recitations.

Wrote article for Intelligencer etc.

Filled orders for Dutch Tracts.

Mission Circle Met as usual.

2

October, Wednesday 31. 1888.

Attended Recitations.

Preaching & Society of Inquiry in evening.

Reports of delegates.

A good spirit prevailed. Many seemed filled with the spirit of Paul's "What will thou have me to do?".

At 10 P.M. I had a pleasant talk with Cantine & Phelps on what constitutes a call to the Foreign field & we prayed to-gether.

Oh how sweet is Xtian fellowship.

November 1888

November, Thursday 1. 1888.

Attended Recitations.

Spent P.M. & Evening in study & writing letters etc.

Felt a nearness & a blessedness of Divine Presence such as Never before.

Read Finney's[1] Power from on High which impressed me very much.

$$\mathcal{G}$$

November, Friday 2. 1888.

Attended Recitations.

Taught French pupil as usual. To-day is last lesson as he returns to Princeton. When he pays me I will be able to pay my debts again. Spent P.M. in study called on J.T. Demarest.

Commenced to pray & work to form a Y.P.S.C.E. in our church.

I trust I shall succeed. Mr. Johnson called on me this evening.

Wrote article for De Hope on Brazil.

Retired late.

$$\mathcal{G}$$

November, Saturday 3. 1888.

Studied, Read & sent article to Press.

Called on Mr. Johnson in P.M. at 85 Murrell St.

Pleasant weather.

$$\mathcal{G}$$

November, Sunday 4. 1888.

Attended services in A.M. at Suydam St. Prayer Meeting in my room —

---

[1] Charles Grandison Finney (1792-1875), Presbyterian Minister, President, Oberlin College 1851-1866. https://en.wikipedia.org/wiki/Charles_Grandison_Finney.

Was asked by Dr. Campbell to speak this P.M. on Missions; accepted..

Taught S.S. class & spoke to them about joining church.

Spoke on Missions for 20 minutes to our church especially touching upon t<u>rue</u> mo<u>tives</u>.

Young Peoples Prayer-Meeting. Heard Rev. Hutton D.D. in evening

Good sermon on <u>Isaiah</u> 66:13. —
Had a talk with Will Chamberlain[2] & retired.

November, Monday 5. 1888.

Attended recitations in P.M. & spent A.M. in Study & Bible Reading.

Am reading Ezekiel at present — full of difficulties & beauties.

Had lesson in Elocution by Prof. Peabody in afternoon.

Saw Political Parade in evening.

Received some more orders for my leaflet on Missions —

November, Tuesday 6. 1888.

Attended Recitations except Dr. Lansing who excused us because of Election day.
Voted my first ticket — (see back of diary)
Voted for Third Party for following reasons:

1. I am against anti-Chinese legislation.
2. The Republican Party has not recognized the chains of temperance & is in secret league with t<u>he Rum</u> Power.

Am much censured for voting as I did. Time will tell.
Bible Class in Dr. Mabon's Room.

[2]   William Isaac Chamberlain (1862-1937), Missionary to India, 1887-1905. HD, 65

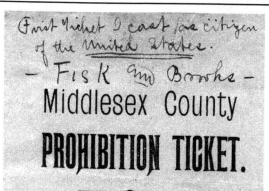

(First Ticket I cast for citizen of the United States.

— FISK and Brooks —

Middlesex County

PROHIBITION TICKET.

SECOND ASSEMBLY DISTRICT

Electors at Large,
CLAYTON LIPPINCOTT,
DAVID F. MERRITT,

District Electors,
THOMAS ANNADOWN,
CHARLES B. COLES,
THEODORE W. BURGER,
WILLIAM H. MORROW,
CHARLES H. STOCKING,
STEPHEN FRANCISCO,
ROBERT R. DOHERTY.

For Representative in Congress,
NOEL R. PARK.

For Senator,
JAMES G. CORTELYOU.

For Coroners,
J. B. HARRIS,
E. ARTHUR HULTS.

For Member of Assembly,
JOSEPH HORNER,

Samuel Zwemer's voting ticket for
Middlesex County, New Jersey.

3

November, Wednesday 7. 1888.

[No Entry]

૭

November, Thursday 8. 1888.

Heard Chaplain Mc Cabe this eve. on Missions & also Rev. Baldwin — both promised to come & speak for our <u>Mission</u> Circle.

૭

November, Friday 9. 1888.

Spoke to Y.P. Union about forming a Young Peoples Soc. of Christian Endeavor for our church.

૭

November, Saturday 10. 1888.

Spent A.M. in writing & study.

Train at 10:43 A.M. for New York.

Heavy Rain all day. Called at Mission Rooms & also at Methodist Mission Rooms 805 Broadway.

Took train for Paterson N.J. where I am to speak to-morrow on Missions.

Was cordially welcomed by Rev. Nies Called on Rev. Huysoon[3] & Rev. Van't Liv[4]

૭

November, Sunday 11. 1888.

Spoke in Rev. Nies' church in A.M. -
good audience. Was not allowed to hang my missy map as the Consistory (objected!) Spoke nevertheless. Good collection $31. Spoke in Rev. Huyssoons [Huysoon] church in P.M. & in their S.S.

In Rev. Van t Liv's church in evening used map in both cases. Was greatly helped in my work by My Leader – who is indeed "a present help in time of need."

[3] James Huysoon (1823-1894), Pastor First Holland, Paterson, NJ, 1868-1892. HD, 191
[4] Possibly Elbert Van Hetloo who served at Sixth Holland, Paterson, NJ, 1888-1905. HD, 425

A Blessed Sabbath.
[Spoke on Acts 16:9]

§

November, Monday 12. 1888.

Took train for N.Y. at 8:10 – Received seven dollars for my services yesterday Handed the collections to the Board. $65. Attended Recitations Met Miss. Pundit a Missy. from India returned on account of ill health.

Had pleasant talk with her in parlor.

§

November, Tuesday 13. 1888.

Attended Recitations & Bible Class of Dr. Mabons. Pleasant meeting of the Mission Circle.

Prof. Woodbridge addressed us in subject of Persona Call to Foreign Field.

(Had a talk with James Cantine in evening & he says he will go to Foreign Field.

God has answered my prayers.)

§

November, Wednesday 14. 1888.

Attended Recitations – Studied & wrote letters in P.M.
Meeting of Soc. of Inquiry in evening. Collected term dues —

Debate this evening very interesting on the use & abuse of the Y.M.C.A.

Had a short talk with Phelps & Cantine on the choice of a field of work.

We spoke of the idea of forming a self- supporting Mission of the Reformed Church.

Is it possible?
Had an hour of prayer. on the subject.

Philip Tertius Phelps

ℨ

November, Thursday 15. 1888.

Attended Recitations-

Called on Dr. Lansing with Mr. Phelps. Spoke of practicability of starting a Mission in Arabia independent of church Boards. He seemed to favor it.

After social hour we left; all resolving to think & pray over the matter again.

Retired late after a meeting of prayer & consultation in Mr. Phelps room.

ℨ

November, Friday 16. 1888.

Recitations as usual. Weather wet & cold all week.
Spent P.M. in Bible-Study & letter writing.

Went to Y. People Union with Miss. Corwin in evening.

Pleasant walk & talk. Meeting poorly attended.

As President I urged them to greater effort & suggested the formation of a Soc. of Xtian Endeavor such as find so much success in other churches.

Retired late. 11:50

🎜

November, Saturday 17. 1888.

Spent day in writing for press & reading —

Mended pair of pants in P.M.

Purchased some postage requisites & wrote several letters.
To Chaplain Mc Cabe to get him to address our Mission Circle etc. Evening in writing & Bible Study.

🎜

November, Sunday 18. 1888.

Arose early. Prayer Meeting in my room. 7 present Attended 1st Meeting of Young Peoples Prayer Meeting at Suydam St. 10 A.M. Good. Fine & telling sermon by Dr. Campbell in A.M. on the words: "Let your moderation be known to all men the Lord is at hand" In P.M. taught my S.S. class. One of them expects to join church! Dr. Mabon preached in P.M. on words "Prepare to Meet thy God". Strong & piercing.

Went to Throop Ave in evening. Good attendance at mission.

Carried home Maggie Sebolt[5] who had a falling fit. Helped her mother — Retired late — tired.

🎜

November, Monday 19. 1888.

Spent A.M. in study & writing.
Attended Recitations & Elocutionary Drill by Prof. Peabody —

Spent evening in study & took walk to town — Purchased Stationary etc.

🎜

[5] Margaret Sebolt (1873-1913), child parishoner of Second Reformed Church in New Brunswick, sister of Adeline Sebolt.www.myheritage.com/research/record-1-295059711-4-627/margaret-sebolt-in-myheritage-family-trees

November, Tuesday 20. 1888.

Attended Recitations.

Made a list of all the Missionaries who graduated from our Seminary & framed it & hung it in Committee Room.

Attended Meeting of Mission Circle & was appointed on Library Committee.

Pleasant meeting altho Rev. Ballagh from Japan disappointed us.

Attended preparatory lecture in Suydam St. Church this evening & had pleasure of seeing Maggie Sebolt one of my pupils join church Again an answer to prayer & first - fruits of this year.

Retired after reading Bible.

§

November, Wednesday 21. 1888.

Attended Recitations. Prayer-Meeting was good subject – Abiding in Christ

Studied, Read & wrote at Dutch translation.

Purchased two books — Pilgrim's Progress — & gave them to Lily Fletcher & Maggie Sebolt my S.S. Scholar as they will join church on Sunday.

Led meeting at Throop Ave in evening & spoke on the Bible & Bible Study I trust many were helped to new efforts — at least so they told me.

Had a cup of coffee & cake down town from Mr. Hieber as it was very cold. Retired late.

§

November, Thursday 22. 1888.

Attended Recitations & spent day in study & writing — .

Called on Dr. Corwin in evening & had very pleasant time-

§

November, Friday 23. 1888.

Attended Recitations —

Called with Phelps & Cantine on Dr. Lansing in reference to the self-supporting Mission plan.
Have volunteered to join it.
Spent evening in study & went to Y.M.C.A. meeting with Chas. Corwin.

Rev. Lamb — Evangelist is an earnest & faithful worker of fine appearance & with a good voice for singing etc.

Retired late.

9
$

November, Saturday 24. 1888.

Prepared lessons for Monday. Read Theology.

Took train at 10:19 A.M. for New York. Called at Mission Rooms —
Also at 440 Lexington Ave on Dr. C S Durand[6] who will speak for the Mission Circle on Tuesday in Dec.

Dinner at Restaurant. Boat for Staten Island. Welcome reception at Mrs. C.B. Hortons.
Supper & Conversation on the West. —
She is very active for Missions.

Dr. Brownlee[7] & Rev. Demarest[8] are jointly pastors of the church at Port Richmond.

9
$

November, Sunday 25. 1888.

Attended S.S. in A.M. taught a class of men & spoke on Missions using maps etc.
Heard a good sermon by Rev. Demarest on <u>Patience</u>. Dinner.
Took train for Erastina — S. School in P.M.

[6] Charles S. Durand, medical missionary to Hurda, India.
[7] James Brownlee (1808-1895), Pastor, Staten Island, NY, 1835-1895. HD, 53
[8] Alfred Howard Demarest (1860-1904), Pastor, Port Richmond, Staten Island, NY, 1884-1901. HD, 96

Addressed School.

Small Attendance on a͟c of severity of snow & storm. The waves on the West Shore were lashed into foam.

Pleasant tea-time.

Attended Service in evening — Dr. Brownlee on text "choose you this day whom you will serve."

Retired early. Very stormy.

Presented Dr. Brownlee with a copy of Father's Poems.

§

November, Monday 26. 1888.

Attended Recitation's as usual.

Spent evening in study.

On my way from New York this A.M. I attended a Medical Lecture by Dr. Keech. on Materia Medica —

§

November, Tuesday 27. 1888.

Attended Recitations.

No meeting of Mission Circle.

Spent evening in writing & study —

§

November, Wednesday 28. 1888.

Recitations as usual.

Went to a cottage Prayer Meeting with Mr. Keeling in evening good meeting. Much cause for Thanksgiving.

Was greatly blessed in speaking a few words on the reasons for Thanksgiving & thanks-living for God.

Retired late.

§

November, Thursday 29. 1888.

Thanksgiving-day! Sermon in A.M. by Rev. Packman. Too much Proclamation of the Pres. & not enough Gospel thankfulness. Enjoyed it however.

Dinner at the Hall. Mr. & Mrs. Corwin did all in their power to make it pleasant for us. Games after dinner.

Social hour in the Parlor. Dr. Lansing gave me $25 as a xmas-present to-day!

Needed it very much.

Spent evening in games etc. in the parlor of Rev. Corwin.

$$\mathcal{Z}$$

November, Friday 30. 1888.

A.M. in writing & answering letter & straightening accounts.

Sent packages of Missy literature to different Societies in **our** church.

Enjoyed the Noon – day hour of prayer.

Spent evening in study & reading.

Attended Y.M.C.A. Meeting for Young Men & distributed invitations in the Saloons etc.

Retired late.

This has been a busy day

December 1888

December, Saturday 1. 1888.

Spent A.M. in writing an article on Missions for "De Hope" & in finishing the Translation of "Sketch of our Mission in China" into Dutch.

Went to town in afternoon. Made some purchases.

Spent evening in writing & reading.
Dr. Lansing called on me.
Took bath & retired.

$$\mathcal{3}$$

December, Sunday 2. 1888.

Morning fine. Had prayer-meeting in my room. 7 present. Attended church in A.M. Communion Season. One of my S.S. scholars joined church. (Maggie Sebolt); poor girl had one of her fainting attacks again. Helped her home. Walked home from church with Mrs. Corwin & had a pleasant talk.

S.S. in P.M. all my class except Maggie present.

Went to cottage-prayer-meeting in P.M. & was greatly blessed. Life among the lowly is often near to Christ.

Led evening prayers at the Hall.

Attended 1st Ref. Ch in evening & heard Mr. Sev. Cotton on Home Missions.

$$\mathcal{3}$$

December, Monday 3. 1888.

Recitations & Study —

$$\mathcal{3}$$

December, Tuesday 4. 1888.

Recitations as usual.

Rev. J. F. Ritts failed to meet the mission circle at 4 P.M. but came later.

Addressed the students in the chapel.

Pleasant talker. He is a pioneer in Medical Missy of the Baptist Church in Northern China.

Spent a social hour in the Parlor with him.

Retired late.

♫

December, Wednesday 5. 1888.

Attended Recitations — Prayer Meeting at noon.

Attended meeting of the Society of Inquiry in evening & took part in debate.

Read & wrote letters.

♫

December, Thursday 6. 1888.

Attended all the Recitations.
Spent P.M. in reading & writing for "De Hope" etc.

Called on Dr. Woodbridge with Mr. Phelps in evening. Pleasant time. Wrote article for the Mission Field on "What do our Church Standards say on Missions?"
Retired late.

♫

December, Friday 7. 1888.

Went to all lectures except Dr. Lansing who was un-well.

Took train at 2:20 P.M. for New York. Called at Synod's Rooms & went to Medical Institute Supper. Pleasant chat with Briggs, Wanless, & Kitts.
Took elevated R.R. for Union Theol. Seminary.

Met Stoops & Wilder—went with Stoops to "American Industrial Institute" Pleasant & Profitable visit.
Prayer-meeting & Council in Wilder's Room. Good-day & Good night. 12.40 A.M.

♫

December, Saturday 8. 1888.

Arose at 7.30. Breakfast with Stoops.

Went to several bookstores etc for shopping—

Called at M.E. & Pres. For. Missy Board Rooms for literature etc.

Train at 4.00 P.M. for Linden was met at depot by Mr. D. Demot & entertained at his home.

Pleasant people.

Little Besaie is a peculiar girl.

All are social & kind.

Attended Xmas Rehearsal in evening—

December, Sunday 9. 1888.

Preached at Linden N.J. A.M. I Cor.15:58 — Small attendance but very attentive. I was greatly helped in my speaking!

S School in P.M. taught the Bible-Class.

Preached on Missions in evening. Was helpd & blessed "exceedingly abundantly" —

Good collection.

Spent evening in conversation with Mr. Demot etc.

December, Monday 10. 1888.

Train for New Brunswick at 7.30. Studied & letters Attended Recitations.

Weather wet & disagreeable—

Spent evening in reading & writing letters, after Dr. Meyer's lecture on the Fall.

(see Lectures 1888-89)

The Lawn-Tennis club have their oyster-supper this evening.

Retired late, after reading my Bible.

December, Tuesday 11. 1888.

[No Entry]

Lewis Curry Andrew

❦

December, Wednesday 12. 1888.

Dr. Baldwin of the M.E. Church addressed / Mission Circle to-day – Very interesting

Met Secty of Y.M.C.A. & agreed to do "Slum" work among the Saloons this winter.

❦

December, Thursday 13. 1888.

[No Entry]

❦

December, Friday 14. 1888.

Supply pulpit for classmate Andrew. Took train for New York. Thence to West Farms where I led prayer-meeting—
Spoke with an inquirer.
Am staying with Mr. Squires.

9
7

December, Saturday 15. 1888.

Spent day in New York etc.
Called at Synod Rooms
Purchased some "Xmas Gifts—
Studied & wrote letters—
Called on Mr. Fitch—elder in evening.
Retired late—

9
7

December, Sunday 16. 1888.

Arose at 7 A.M.
Breakfast. S.School.
Took Bible Class. Lesson on Sampson.
Preached Missy. Sermon in A.M. on Prov. 24:12.

Went to Peabody Home for aged women & spoke there in P.M.
Called on Mr. Schrverki. Spoke on Missions in the Presbyterean Ch in evening at 7.
Preached in Ref. Ch at 7.30 on Math 27: "Sitting down they watched Him there".
Was greatly helped all day.

God's mercies are wonderful & his power marvellous.

9
7

December, Monday 17, 1888.

Train at 6 A.M. for New York—

Gave Missy Collection $8.50 to Rev. Cobb D.D. Train for New Brunswick. Studied & Recited.

Read & Studied in P.M.
1st Lecture of Missy course in Seminary this evening by Rev. Stout[1] of Japan.
Quite Good.

---

[1] Henry Stout (1838-1912), Missionary, South Japan, 1869-1906. HD, 379

૭

December, Tuesday 18. 1888.

Attended Recitations as usual.

૭

December, Wednesday 19. 1888.

Attended all Recitations Meet v [of] Soc v [of] Inq. In even/g —
Resigned posi- as treasurer.
Attended Cottage-Prayer-Meetg with Mr. Keeling—
Was greatly blessed.
Spoke on Prodigal Son.

૭

December, Thursday 20. 1888.

Attended Recitations as usual—
Spent P.M. in study—
Called on Dr. Drury & received several small volumes as pay for
work as Correspondent to the Xtian Intelligencer.

Commenced work in Saloons of city on invitation v [of] Y.M.C.A.
Secty Hines accompanied me.
Had a cordial reception in most places — surprised! One saloon
had the motto: "In God we trust—all others must pay"!
Met 89 young men & distributed tracks & Y.M.C.A. Invitations—
Retired late—

૭

December, Friday 21. 1888.

Attended final Recita's Prof. De Witt was very pleasant.
Decided not to go with Phelps to Blenheim N.Y.
Studied & wrote article for the Press.

Spent P.M. in calling & correspondence.
Attended Y. P. Union in company with Miss. Corwin — pleasant
time & the business meeting.
Pleasant walk home in the moonlight.
Retired after a game of Checkers - Miss. C. is champion—

॰ॄ

December, Saturday 22. 1888.

Called on Addie Sebolt[2] this A.M. Maggie is still sick — poor child — she gave me a bunch of wax flowers for Xmas.

Settled Bank account & took train at 12:55 for New York.
Purchased New overcoat at Hacket & Co — $10 Not stylish nor beautiful but very serviceable.

Boat for Ft. Lee.
Pleasant time with Miss. Person at the old homestead on the Palisades—
Called on Rev. Buckelew[3] in evening—
Was asked to preach. Accepted—
Read Bible & retired

॰ॄ

December, Sunday 23. 1888.

Arose late — Very cold. Attended Church & heard sermon by Rev. Buckelew on "The Magi". Dinner at Persons. S.S. in P.M. Taught Bible Class—
Read Genesis 1-6 with Miss. Person for study.

Supper Attended Church & preached on the Death of Christ "Sitting down they watched him there". Was helped in speaking. Read Bible, Conversa - & retired.

॰ॄ

December, Monday 24. 1888.

Arose early. Boat for New York. Spent day in sight-seeing.
Visited Wall-Street & Trinity — attended Meet v [of] Pastor's Association & heard paper by Rev. Searle's[4] on subject "Egypt in August".

[2] Adeline Sebolt Selover (1877-1946), child parishoner of Second Reformed Church in New Brunswick, sister of Margaret Sebolt. MH; https://www.findagrave.com/memorial/84461176/adeline-selover
[3] William Dey Buckelew (1825-1893), Pastor, Schoharie Mountain, NY, 1879-1889. HD, 56
[4] John Preston Searle (1854-1922), Pastor, First, Raritan, Somerville, NJ, 1881-93. HD, 354

Moritz Johannes Schwartz

Heard Dr. Dix in P.M. at Trinity—
Episcopalians v [of] that type are more than half Romish. Deliver me from such "Divine Service"!
Walked down Broadway & up to to 14th Street.
Train for New Brunswick. Called on Corwins'.

☙

December, Tuesday 25. 1888.

Xmas day! Received $5.00 by mail from Father & other presents—
Letters from home—
Received Xmas Card at Breakfast from the Corwins.
Attended Catholic Church with Charlie Corwin[5].
Dinner Candy-pull — very interesting & extensive in character, games etc.

Called in the Parlor in the evening.
Played Mr. Schwartz[6] a game of Chess.
Song & Candy.
A Merry Xmas indeed.

---

[5]   Charles Edward Corwin (1868-1958), Rutgers College, 1892. Son of E. T. Corwin. HD, 79
[6]   Moritz Johannes Schwartz (1853-?), New Brunswick Theological Seminary, 1890. Raven 160

♒

December, Wednesday 26. 1888.

Spent day in writing & reading.
Wrote article for "De Hope" on Missions & for the Mission Field.

Evening at the "Y Mission" for Drunkards—
Led meeting — played the organ — subject "Giving & Receiving at Xmas". John 3:16 - Math 2:1-14
Gave Candy & Oranges to the children at the Mission.
Long talk in Keeling's Room. He is a fine fellow & does hard service in the vineyard

♒

December, Thursday 27. 1888.

Arose late. Read some in Augustine's[7] Confessions this morning—
A strangely interesting book. How he addresses God as a child his father & conceals nothing from him.
Read & Studied a little. Prepared an address for Throop Ave. Mission.

Went to Suydam St. Ch Rehearsal with Miss. Corwin & from there to Throop Avenue.
Spoke at the meeting — she sang a Solo.
Rode home in tears
Pleasant company & good evening in every respect.
Had some candy-taffy in the parlor. /——

♒

December, Friday 28. 1888.

Arose at 6.30. Spent A.M. in answering correspondence & other work—
Walk down town—
Call on Dr. Woodbridge.
Attended S.S. Entertainment at Suydam St. Church—
Large attendance—

[7] Augustine of Hippo, Bishop of Hippo, 396-430. *Britannica* 15th Ed. v14, 397

Received 6 hand chiefs—
a Xmas present from James Mabon—
Walked home with Miss. Corwin. — Pleasant conversation—
Maggie Sebolt — my S.S. scholar had a falling fit again this evening—
　　helped her home—
　　Retired late.

♃

December, Saturday 29. 1888.

Studied in A.M. —
took bath etc—
Train at 3:52 for Jersey City—
Am to preach at the Free Reformed in reply to a despatch from Rev. A.A. Zabriskie[8] to supply pulpit
Was warmly welcomed at Mrs. Zabriskie—

Game of chess in evening. Interesting children—
Jennie & Harry.

Retired after reading Scripture & prayer for success on the morrow.

♃

December, Sunday 30. 1888.

Arose late. Attended service in A.M. & spoke on John 8:12—
Was quite free in my delivery — but dislike to read sermons—

Dinner at Zabriskies—
Called on Alfred Duncombe in P.M. & found him some better — He has had severe spell of sickness.
Also on Dr. Van Cleef & Mrs. Pleasant talk with her on Missions & Raising funds—
Preached in evening before large number of young people — Math 27: "Sitting down they watched Him there"
Was helped but did not feel as free as last sabbath___

♃

---

[8]　Albert Ashleigh Zabriskie (1843-1922), Pastor, Free, Jersey City, NJ, 1887-91. HD, 477

December, Monday 31. 1888.

Last day in the year!_
Arose early — Read a review of the year's <u>news</u> in "the Congrega'alis"

Train for New Brunswick at 11 A.M. after some shopping & receiving $5.00 & expenses for my services—

P.M. at the Hall—
Called on Dr. Corwin's in the evening & remained with them to watch out the Old year. Chimes —Song — Candy — Thoughts
      (for 1888)
Read Diary ^ at 12:30 — & retired—

Welcome <u>1889</u>!

Amy Zwemer and Samuel Zwemer with child.

10275855R00115

Made in the USA
Lexington, KY
25 September 2018